PANTRY AND PALATE

REMEMBERING AND REDISCOVERING ACADIAN FOOD

WITH A FOREWORD BY NAOMI DUGUID

PANTRY *AND* PALATE

REMEMBERING AND REDISCOVERING ACADIAN FOOD

SIMON THIBAULT

PHOTOS BY NOAH FECKS

NIMBUS
PUBLISHING LTD
nimbus.ca

Nimbus Publishing Limited
3731 Mackintosh St, Halifax, NS, B3K 5A5
(902) 455-4286 nimbus.ca

Printed and bound in Canada
Design: Kate Westphal, Graphic Detail Inc.

NB1209

Library and Archives Canada Cataloguing in Publication

Thibault, Simon, 1976-, author
Pantry and palate : remembering and rediscovering Acadian food / text by Simon Thibault ; fo-
reword by Naomi Duguid ; and photos by Noah Fecks.
Includes bibliographical references and index.
ISBN 978-1-77108-490-1 (softcover)

1. Cooking, Acadian. 2. Acadians. 3. Thibault, Simon, 1976- —Family. 4. Cookbooks. I. Duguid,
Naomi, writer of foreword II. Fecks, Noah, photographer III. Title.

TX715.6.T533 2017   641.59715   C2016-908020-X

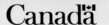

Nimbus Publishing acknowledges the financial support for its publishing activities from the
Government of Canada, the Canada Council for the Arts, and from the Province of Nova Scotia.
We are pleased to work in partnership with the Province of Nova Scotia to develop and promote our
creative industries for the benefit of all Nova Scotians.

Pour mes aieux. Deux familles, un palais, un dorsoir.
For those who came before me. Two families, one palate, one pantry.

For Sophie and Ella. *'Noncle Simon vous aimes beaucoup.*

And for Ginette Thibault-Halman, my sister, my accomplice, my hero.

CONTENTS

MAPS OF ACADIE

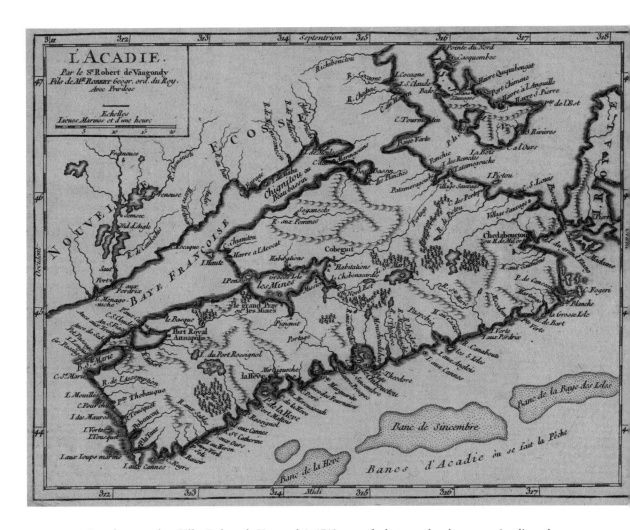

French mapmaker Gilles Robert de Vaugondy's 1748 map of what was then known as Acadie and is now known as the Canadian Maritime provinces of Nova Scotia, New Brunswick, and Prince Edward Island. NOVA SCOTIA ARCHIVES

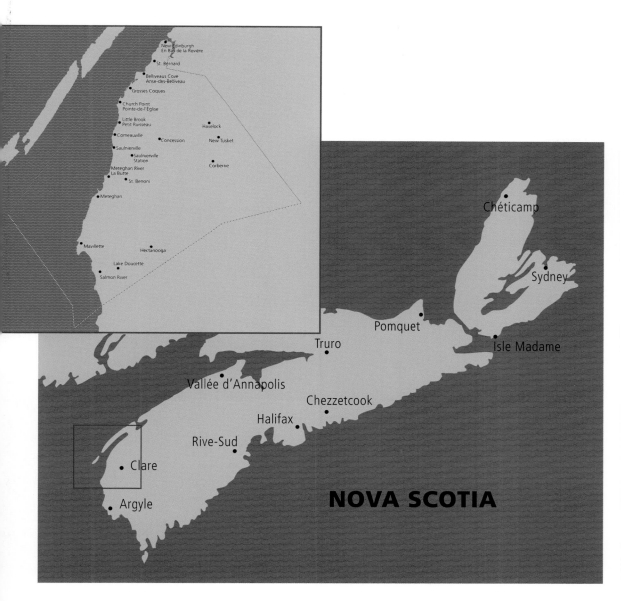

New Edinburgh
En Bas de la Rivière
St. Bernard
Beliveaus Cove
Anse-des-Beliveau
Grosses Coques
Church Point
Pointe-de-l'Église
Little Brook
Petit Ruisseau
Havelock
Comeauville
Concession
New Tusket
Saulnierville
Saulnierville
Station
Corberrie
Meteghan River
La Butte
St. Benoni
Meteghan

Mavillette
Hectanooga
Lake Doucette
Salmon River

Chéticamp

Sydney

Pomquet

Truro

Isle Madame

Vallée d'Annapolis

Chezzetcook

Halifax

Rive-Sud

Clare

NOVA SCOTIA

Argyle

Acadian communities of Nova Scotia. Inset: Clare, La Baie Sainte-Marie.

CANADIAN
MASON
JAR

tdsp. vanilla + salt.

Beat eggs until frothy, a[dd]
[su]gar + beat well. (a little su[gar]
[a]t a time) Add to other ingredi[ents]
[s]hape into small cookies. Bake
slow ...

FOREWORD

Until I read this book, like most Canadians I had very little knowledge of Acadian foodways. I knew the Acadians were the earliest European settlers in Canada, people who had come from France in the seventeenth century and settled and prospered in "L'Acadie" in fertile areas of present-day Nova Scotia and New Brunswick. I had read about their long and often tragic history, especially their expulsion from their lands by English conquerors in the course of the eighteenth century. Many Acadians fled to Louisiana, where their cuisine evolved into what we now call "Cajun." Others hung on in more remote, less fertile parts of Nova Scotia and New Brunswick.

And it is the food of those Acadians, especially those in Nova Scotia, that Simon Thibault brings us in this graceful, generous book.

Foodways are an expression of history and culture, and of identity. They're the product of human ingenuity as it responds to climate and terrain, trade connections, community history, and religious beliefs. And we can always learn a great deal from studying them.

That's why this book about Acadian food culture is so important and so fascinating. In it we learn about the tenacity of Acadian food traditions and the way they have evolved.

We are given this privileged access by an author who is not an interested outsider but instead a committed and passionate insider. Like his parents and generations of his forebears, Simon Thibault is a proud member of the Acadian community of Nova Scotia. This book is a product of his deep commitment to understanding Acadian food traditions and to preserving and celebrating them.

As he sleuths his way through the extraordinary notebooks left behind by his grandmother and other relatives, finds treasures and insights in early scholarly works on Acadian history and culture, and interrogates members of his community about their food memories and insights, he's a participant as well as an investigator. He laces the nuggets he gleans with his childhood memories of dishes such as *râpure* and *fricot*, and in some cases suggests appealing updated takes on family dishes.

The recipes are distinctive, as if from a far-off land, and yet also accessible. They feel like a direct transmission of the wisdom of Acadian cooks from generations past. It is our good fortune that they have been retrieved and gracefully interpreted by a modern-day insider to the tradition.

Naomi Duguid

Naomi Duguid is an award-winning food writer and cookbook author, having won numerous James Beard Foundation Awards for her cookbooks. She is is often described as a culinary anthropologist. Her most recent book, *Taste of Persia: A Cook's Travels Through Armenia, Azerbaijan, Georgia, Iran, and Kurdistan*, was published in September 2016.

Tourtière, or meat pie,
recipe on page 133

4 sq. melted chocolate or
7-8 Tablespoons cocoa.
2 eggs.
2 cups Bread Flour
2 tsp. B. Powder.
1 cup canned milk (whole)
2 cups nutmeats

Macaroons.

2 cups Corn Flakes
1 " cocoanut
1 " sugar.
2 egg whites beaten stiff
1 tbsp. vanilla & salt.

Beat eggs until frothy, add
sugar & beat well. (a little sugar
at a time) Add other ingredients
Shape into small cookies. Bake in
a slow oven.

Cookies au Beurre.

1 tasse de beurre

Party Cake.

1 cup sugar
½ a shortening } cream.
Pinch of salt
¾ cups milk
1 teas. cream tartar

1½ cups flour
7 lover.

Lastly 2
unbeaten eggs.

PREFACE

The Comeau Women, or How I Came to Write this Cookbook

Like all good stories, this one has more than one beginning.

You could say it started over one hundred years ago, or maybe just two years ago. You could say it started when my grandfather preserved every scrap of written material that had his family's touch, or maybe it started when my mother gave me a gift of old notebooks saved by her own father. It all depends on how you want to look at it.

I started living this story when I found myself washing dirty pots in the tiny kitchen of my apartment. My hands were greased with rendered pork fat, an ingredient and process I had not indulged in before. It's not the most immediately appetizing of scenarios, but indulge me.

My father goes hunting during the fall, and he often brings me all sorts of game when he and my mother come to visit: brown paper bundles of deer roasts, cleaned and segmented wild hare, the occasional partridge. I've taken it upon myself to learn to cook these meats properly so as not to waste them, as I find myself very lucky to have access to wild game. Thankfully, I have a decent-sized collection of cookbooks, with recipes of food from around the world, and in one of them is a recipe for rabbit *rillettes*—a type of French pâté—that I'd been wanting to try for years. I decided to substitute hare—a much more flavoursome meat—and make the dish for the first time.

The recipe asked for rendered pork fat, and so I learned how to render my own. It was surprisingly easy, and if you stay tuned, I'll show you how. (*Didn't I just say that good stories have more than one beginning? So do most recipes.*)

I had read the recipe multiple times to make sure I didn't forget anything. I followed the steps and felt proud that I had been able to execute the recipe, not to mention excited about serving it at Christmas for the family. Like all good recipes and endeavours, there was also a lot of cleaning to do. My hands were covered in the now-seasoned pork fat, and so I turned on the tap and placed my hands under the running water, waiting for it to warm up.

As I rubbed my hands under the slowly warming water, it beaded over them, falling like tiny clear ball bearings into the sink. My skin was impregnable to the water. I took my hands out and looked at them, rubbing them together and feeling the thin layer of fat spread as it warmed from the heat of my hands. What could easily be viewed as an unpleasant feeling became the basis for a moment of quiet reflection. It left me wondering if this sensation—which was once well known to many a home cook—had become a little lost, as if it had wandered off, finding occasional homes amongst hardcore bakers and amateur butchers. I wondered if my grandmothers, and every other woman who would have been cooking less than a century ago, would have known this feeling or taken it as a messy necessity. I knew the answer, and I told myself I would respect it.

You see, I'd been thinking about my grandmothers a lot, especially my maternal grandmother, Rosalie. I never really knew her, as she passed away when I was four, and I have no real memories of her. I'd been told stories of her, how she was an intelligent woman in a time when intelligent women were often neglected. Thanks to a family member, she was lucky and sent to study *les arts ménager* (or home economics) at a women's college in Trois-Rivières, Québec.

A few years ago, knowing that I was interested in cookery in all its forms, my mother loaned me a series of old family notebooks. "This one was my mother's,"

My grandparents, Augustin (*à Étienne à Justinien*) and Rosalie (*à Théophile à Maximin*), on their wedding day, August 11, 1936. COURTESY OF AUTHOR

she said, pointing out the distinct cursive that filled the lines of one small notebook with a false leather cover. As I flipped through it, I recognized another's handwriting midway through the book: my own mother's. "I wanted to learn to cook when I was a teenager, so *Mame* let me write recipes in her book," she said.

We dug through the other three notebooks, and she recognized another as having her mother's writing, but she was at first unsure as to who wrote the other two. "This looks like Marianne's handwriting," she said, hesitating and remembering. "Marianne was Eulalie and Séraphin's daughter, and my father was raised alongside of Marianne like a sister, even though they were cousins." There are occasional names written down inside the notebooks, citing where the recipes came from: names I'd heard in passing over the years when Mom would talk about her own family; names that were common one hundred years ago in French-speaking areas of rural Nova Scotia. Agnès. Emélie. Séraphin. Marie Rose. Jeanne. The "anne" in Marianne was pronounced with a lengthy "awn," like in lawn, as was the "anne" in Jeanne. Times change, names change, methods of cooking change, and the ways of writing recipes changes, but certain things linger; memories, like flavours on our tongues.

Sitting at my kitchen table, a step or two away from my grease-tinged hands, was a record of the cooking of these women, written down in notebooks of now-yellowed paper. Some of the notebooks are no bigger than my hand. Some of them have lost their binding, their pages on the verge of falling out. They became very precious to me as I began to cook from them.

I went deeper into the family notebooks, and I found recipes that gave their user a list of ingredients with varying scales of measurement and accuracy. I found notes and recipes created and transcribed by women who had spent years in kitchens. They only needed the smallest of references to remind them how to do things: these recipes were almost second nature. Directions were spotty, if they were included at all.

I had my work cut out for me.

The more I cooked and the more I baked, the more I figured out the missing pieces of these recipes. I came to revere these Acadian women and other women like them. I started digging elsewhere for more recipes like these in an old ladies' auxiliary cookbook and from other Acadian regions in the Maritimes. Eventually I had enough to make up the contents of this book; it is devoted to the collective and semi-collected works of women who cooked for and amidst generations of Acadians.

This book is all about understanding, learning, and respecting the kitchens, pantries, and palates of those who came before me. In creating this cookbook, I wanted to access to the past through meals, and gain insight into the flavours and stories of how, what, and why people cooked.

I hope after reading this book that you will not only cook some of these dishes, but perhaps even examine your own family pantry with the same gaze.

A rare photo of Rosalie in her youth, enjoying the snow, date unknown. COURTESY OF AUTHOR

INTRODUCTION

Preserving Family Connections

It's hard to talk about food and not talk about family.

When talking about our favourite dishes, many of us often start by saying that "My grandmother made," or "My [insert family member] made," and then talk about how those particular dishes were made in very particular ways. Those dishes and the way they are made have left indelible marks on our hearts, our bellies, and our souls.

This becomes even more important when a person's culture is different from the one where they reside. The dishes we serve are ways to persevere and preserve. It's another way to look at what noted nineteenth-century French gourmand Jean Anthelme Brillat-Savarin once said: "Tell me what you eat, and I will tell you what you are."

When it comes to telling people who we are, Acadians have for a long time distinguished themselves. We are the descendants of the first French settlers to what is now known as Nova Scotia, New Brunswick, and Prince Edward Island. We were agriculturists who tended to the land, our flocks, our orchards. By the time the mid-1700s rolled around, we no longer considered ourselves to be French citizens. Meanwhile, France and England had been sparring over land in the "New World," and soon the region known as Acadie was under English rule. We were asked to proclaim our loyalty to the English crown. But we were separated by hundreds of miles from France, not to mention dozens of years of calling it our "home," and we simply wanted to be left in peace. The English didn't view that as acceptable, and so, starting in 1755 and for nearly a decade, Acadian families were forcibly removed form their lands. This is what is known by Acadians as *le grand dérangement*. The Deportation. Families were torn apart, separated, and sent to various locales, many of them imprisoned. Although this is a vast over-simplification of a long story, the short version is that some of us did return to what is now known as Nova Scotia, New Brunswick, Prince Edward Island, and even parts of Québec and Maine. Some of us ended up in Louisiana, but that is an even more complex story, one that I will leave to others to tell. When we did return, we were not allowed to return to the lands we had once cultivated. The lands we were granted were often less than desirable, let alone arable. But we persevered. We came in contact with people with various histories and ethnicities, and we adopted some of their foodways as our own. We were resolute. We once again settled in and planted our roots.

Our roots were fed not only by the foodways we kept, but also by the way that we spoke (historically in French, often surrounded by English speakers), and by the way we professed our faith (Catholics amongst Protestants). Like many dispersed cultures, Acadians distinguish and recognize one another through names: names like Comeau, LeBlanc, Doucet, Boudreau. These family names often repeat themselves, and so one Doucet may or may not be related to another, at least not for a few generations. So how does an Acadian figure out which clan he or she belongs to? We name ourselves by naming our ancestors. This goes somewhat further than the oft-said "Who's your father" introduction that happens throughout Atlantic Canada (and arguably most of rural North America). For example, if I were to meet an Acadian for the first time who was from the same region as I am, I would say, I am "*Simon, à Hector à Ulysses à Annie et ma mère est Jeanne-Marie à Augustin à Étienne.*" Simon, son of Hector, son of Ulysses, son of Annie and my mother is Jeanne-Marie, daughter of Augustin, son of Étienne.

I could go back even further: my father would be *Hector à Ulysses à Annie (William) à Célestin à Isidore*. This game of to whom we are begotten isn't just a

A delegation of Acadians and Cajuns meeting at Grand-Pré in 1936. At the far right, bottom row, is the author's great-great uncle, François G. J. Comeau, who, along with Dudley LeBlanc, front row, centre, was instrumental in the reconnection of Acadians and Cajuns. COURTESY OF AUTHOR

series of names. It serves as a reminder and touchstone of our past living among us. For example, Isidore was born in 1800, and there is still a road that bears his name not far from where I grew up. My father still owns land on that road, which was bequeathed to him through generations from the original land grants given to the Acadians in the region of Saint Mary's Bay in Nova Scotia. My mother is *Jeanne-Marie à Augustin à Etienne à Justinien à Vieux Jos à Justinien*. Justinien was born in Péticodiac, New Brunswick, in 1729, and his father, François, was born in Port Royal, in what is now Annapolis Royal, Nova Scotia. His land grant was in the village of Meteghan River, Nova Scotia. For the longest time, Meteghan River was known as Justinien's River. This is how memories exist amongst Acadians: we are walking through a palimpsest of our past every day.

The point of this almost biblical "begat-ing" is that it helps fellow Acadians reconnect. Many times I've used my Acadian family names amongst new introductions, and even old friends, only to find out that I am related to the person I am talking to. Most of the time, the relationship is a few times removed; occasionally it's closer, but that's not the point. The point is that we Acadians have long memories. We're not just naming names, we're reconnecting after centuries of separation.

Cooking and food are immediate and nourishing ways to reconnect and harken back to the past—to memories both individual and collective. I found this out myself while writing this book. It started with conversations with my own family: I'd call my parents for tips on how to properly scald the potatoes for *fricot,* or to ask them if they had ever encountered a particular dish or ingredient. But my connections and conversations went even further than the present: they connected me gastronomically and historically with my past.

I am indebted to the women in my own family that I never really knew, as their work is the foundation of a large number of the recipes in this book. The most prominent of them is Rosalie Comeau, my maternal grandmother. Even though I have next to no memories of her, I learned that she was driven, pretty, and educated. At the age of sixteen, she finished high school early, but she had to wait until she was old enough to enter teacher's college. In the interim her brother Maximin, who happened to be a priest, sent her to l'École des Ursulines in Trois-Rivières, Québec. It was a college for women and was also the oldest learning institution for women in North America. There she learned *les arts ménager,* or home economics, but not in the way we think of home economics today. Her *Manuel de cuisine,* a hearty tome that is now in my possession, is an example of what she learned, from how to make mother sauces to the nutritional value of various cuts of meat. Her education—spiritual, intellectual, and culinary—was thorough, and a source of pride for her.

Because of her education, Rosalie's notebooks are filled with nothing but shorthand notes to remind her what to do when cooking. A dish of scalloped cabbage listed ratios, but there was no mention of the ratios she used for her accompanying white sauce. She just knew the recipe. She knew in which order to add the ingredients to her doughnuts, and she needed no instructions.

In 1936 Rosalie married Augustin Comeau, my maternal grandfather. Augustin had been raised by a woman named Eulalie, or Tante Lalie, as she was known. Lalie, along with her husband, became responsible for young Augustin's daily

Rosalie on her graduation day from l'École des Ursulines in Trois-Rivières, Québec. COURTESY OF AUTHOR

care after his mother died from complications shortly after his birth. He was raised amongst his cousins, notably Agnès, Marianne, and Éddé. At the age of twelve, Augustin moved in with his father, Étienne, who ran a small dry goods store in the village of Meteghan River, or La Butte, as it is commonly known. Augustin would go on to marry Rosalie and raise two children, François and Jeanne-Marie Comeau. As an adult, Augustin became known as the keeper of family history. His office and attic were filled to the brim with family notes, histories, and artifacts. Among some of these is the original deed that granted his ancestor Justinien the title to the land that his house stood on. He also held the family notebooks that would come to form and inspire this book.

Cooking from many of these old recipes wasn't always easy. The majority of the recipes only had a basic list of ingredients, and they rarely included directions, let alone detailed ones. So not only did I have to decipher what to do and in what order, but I also had to figure out how to record that information. It was like having a stilted conversation that was decades long: *You need this much of this, and that much of that. You know what to do.* I was determined to gather the same strength of character and ease in a kitchen that these women had, if only in the smallest of doses. Reading through these impeccably scripted notebooks, I found myself wondering about these recipes: How hot did this oven need to be to bake this cake? (350°F, apparently.) Was it a coincidence that the blood pudding/ sausage recipe was written on the same page as one for doughnuts? (Fresh pig's blood also means fresh pig's fat, enough for deep-frying those wonderful treats.)

At first I didn't know what to do, or at least I didn't know much. Much of my cookery knowledge comes from books I've collected and pored over—as well as accidentally poured ingredients over—in addition to a whole lot of trial and error. I never went to culinary school, and my knife skills are passable at best.

But I was determined. I wanted these foods and practices—including the thriftiness of using and eating what was in the pantry, instead of forgetting it—to be part of my daily cooking and eating habits. It's one thing to know how to render lard or to make rhubarb conserves; it's another thing to use it on a regular basis—to use what you have and not waste it. These women knew how to put together meals with limited and specific ingredients and techniques. This wasn't a question of cooking for fun—this was real home *economics*. I didn't want this knowledge to be forgotten.

In the time that many of these recipes were historically being cooked, baked, and preserved, money and availability of certain foodstuffs could be scarce. Thankfully scarcity is arguably less of a concern today for most homes in North America, or at least it's not a concern in the same way it was before: sugar is cheaper than molasses, and not everything has to be salted within an inch of its former life for it to last the long winter. We can still cook in this manner and learn from it. We can learn the basics and then play along those lines.

So I baked.
I cooked.
I preserved.
I ate.

Lena Comeau serving *pâté a la râpure*, Digby County, Nova Scotia, 1950.

Chicken *fricot* with potato dum
recipe on page 122

You Are Where You Eat

"Authenticity" is a benchmark in the culinary world. I remember hearing Naomi Duguid say that it's difficult to define what "authentic" really is, especially when creating recipes. Her recipe from *Hot Sour Salty Sweet: A Culinary Journey through Southeast Asia* (a book I strongly urge you to also read) is where I learned to make *phô*—an amazing savoury and fragrant Vietnamese soup made from soup bones, a little beef, some noodles, and a few spices. When I am making it at home, I try and stay as close to the spirit of the dish as I understand it to be. This understanding comes from years of eating, making, and researching as much as I can about the intricacies of such an important dish. However, I am not an expert and won't claim to be. But that's not why I make a dish. In making *phô*, in tasting the aromatics in the broth, in understanding the techniques, my intent is to know, understand, and respect as much as I can about the history and the process of making *phô*. What matters is respecting a cuisine, its origins, its makers, and the path it has taken. Appreciation, observation, and a keen ear for what a dish is telling you are as close as you can get to an "authentic" culinary experience.

Over the past decade, my work has given me access to food cultures from all over the world. At first I had a simple interest in learning how to cook certain dishes: I sought out recipes for dishes as disparate as the aforementioned *phô*, or maybe a luscious French torte rich with chocolate. These were the beginnings of my becoming a home cook. But the more I read, the more I cooked, the more I wanted to know. Why were certain ingredients or preparations more prevalent in one area, while others were ignored? It became a fascination. I sought out books, restaurants, cooks, and even the dinner tables of friends. I learned to listen, to taste, and most importantly, to respect.

Food *is* culture, and no matter where people call home, they create it. Some of the most fascinating versions (or visions) of foods can come about when people travel to new homes that aren't like their places of origin. This is why you have Chinese food existing in various manifestations from Peru, to Jamaica, to Macau—all of them distinct in their own iteration. Jewish cookery is incredibly diverse, with variations existing beyond simple historic and geographic (such as Sephardic or Ashkenazy) divides. Food doesn't exist exclusively within borders. A papaya salad that is commonly eaten in Southeast Asia can vary from place to place, whether it is made in an Isaan village in Laos and northeastern Thailand, or by a Hmong family in parts of Vietnam. Food does not recognize borders. It recognizes hunger and satisfaction—physical, emotional, and even spiritual.

In the same way, Acadian food exists outside of geographic limits. Beyond the fact that Acadie does not currently exist as a geographic area, it does exist in the hearts of many people throughout Atlantic Canada, and its reach can be found throughout North America.

Versions of *poutines râpées,* a cherished dish in parts of New Brunswick, can be found throughout parts of Germany and even Scandinavia. I know of a few kitchens in Louisiana where *fricot* is made by both Cajuns and transplanted Acadians. I didn't grow up eating *crêpe*-like buckwheat *ployes* like they do in northern New Brunswick and Maine, and the *poutines râpées* I had growing up in southwestern Nova Scotia were nothing like the ones eaten in New Brunswick. Does that mean that one is more authentically Acadian than another?

Acadians lived amongst people of all sorts of ethnic and cultural backgrounds. A perfect example are the Loyalists—both black and white—who came to populate what became Nova Scotia and New Brunswick in the early 1800s. They brought with them an almost ubiquitous use of cornmeal in staple foods such as breads, both leavened and unleavened. Disparate peoples often become less disparate as time goes on. Intermarrying between the French-speaking, Catholic Acadians and the other communities nearby played a part in the dispersion of foodstuffs and the expansion of palates, while the marrying of other Francophones from other French-speaking regions further dispersed Acadian culture and food. Time can be a great culinary emulsifier.

This book is full of recipes of the Acadian diaspora, and to mark one dish as specifically or authentically Acadian becomes difficult for its purposes. A bread made of molasses and cornmeal may be known as Anadama bread in New England, but in many early twentieth-century Acadian homes, it was simply *pain,* or bread. The history and knowledge of such a bread may be unknown to an Acadian housewife making a bread she only knows as her mother's recipe. It was made and eaten without much thought of where it came from, and it was made for sustenance.

When I told people I was writing a book focusing on Acadian food, they often ased, "What is that?" In fact, it's a question I asked myself for almost two years as this book came to fruition.

Some people know about the big dishes, like *poutines râpées* and rappie pie, or *râpure*. They mention meat pies, or soups like *fricot*. And those are important dishes, but it's difficult to write a book or talk about a cuisine in such a limited scope. It denies and limits a people to just a few dishes, and no food culture exists within a vacuum.

The easy-yet-complicated answer to the question, "What is Acadian food" could be: food that is cooked in Acadian homes. The terms "traditionally" and "historically" can be nebulous and leave someone (like your author) searching for and trying recipes that would have been eaten from the seventeenth and eighteenth centuries all the way to the twenty-first century. That's almost too wide a scope, and times and larders have changed. Also, the palatability of those recipes could be limited.

For *Pantry and Palate*, I decided that the majority of dishes would come from my family notebooks. These dishes would have been found on many Acadian kitchen tables throughout the twentieth century. Some of them were more present at the earlier portion of that era, while others were more common later on. This book is not the penultimate book on Acadian cookery. It's a book of recipes and tips and stories and histories that are incredibly local and somewhat global. It is a book that I hope examines foodways that have been both celebrated and forgotten.

Changes in food preservation, such as refrigeration, and the use of chemical leaveners changed the way many Acadian women—let alone women throughout the Western world—cooked during the early part of the twentieth century. This had the unintended consequence of certain recipes having less of a chance to breathe during the latter part of the century. Bread could rise quickly due to prepackaged yeasts. Vinegars could be bought rather than made. Fats could be bought already rendered and shelf-stable (or substituted with vegetable-based versions).

The convenience and ease of access to foods that were previously viewed as daily or seasonal food chores made those recipes no longer necessary to a household. Eating what was in season and making do with what one had on hand were no longer viewed as necessary evils, but rather became quaint and nostalgic customs in many mid-century homes. The salted and preserved foodstuffs that were laborious mainstays of the summer and fall bounty were no longer seasoned by the sweat and hard work of family members, if made at all.

Foodstuffs—and the cultures that created them—have come to be viewed today as commodities to be bought and traded and occasionally discarded. They are no longer treated as emblems of nourishment. It would be easy to think fondly about bread that is shaped by the hands of a loved one as a daily fuel, but this staple was more of a necessity than emotional sustenance. Food was a chore, with hours, days, and even seasons spent producing and preserving it.

Fewer and fewer of us know how to shape, bake, make, and preserve those items of the past. Thankfully, we have a few things on our side. *Maman* and *Grandmère* may no longer have needed to make hearty breads for everyday supper, but some of them kept at it, perhaps to show affection for their loved ones. Certain foods became special dishes that were doled out on special occasions. Notes were written in notebooks, on recipe cards, and in community cookbooks. It's because of that desire to maintain, remember, and know those flavours that many recipes are still around.

Memories of taste are some of the most powerful, and they are often linked to our memories of love. Some of us are lucky enough to have family notebooks filled with recipes. There are also community cookbooks, published as fundraisers by ladies' auxiliaries and church groups. A few people, like Melvin Gallant and Marielle Cormier-Boudreau, made it their mission to create books about Acadian cuisines, but publications like these are few and far between. Their book *A Taste of Acadie* was a labour of love, as were the many other small-press publications that have come out over the years.

General-interest cookbooks published today tend to be visually heavy and made for people with little to no culinary knowledge. This is important as it teaches people to cook, but makes old recipe notebooks and cards inaccessible to many who would want to learn their secrets. The loss of culinary knowledge is unfortunate.

This book is a compass between two poles: it's a general book of recipes that tells you how to dump and stir, and it also contains some knowledge about why things were cooked in the way they were. This is not just a book for people who have an interest in regional cookery, Acadian history, or perhaps Canadian cookery in general. This is a book for those who want to know how to cook well-cherished recipes, and hopefully look at their own foodways in a different light.

So what is Acadian food? It's food that is humble, homey, occasionally homely, and very comforting. Its history extends through family pantries, meals, recipes, and memories. It is made with love and devotion and from a larder that is small but mighty. It is made to be eaten.

I found this image, from a series of photos taken in the 1950s in Cape Saint Mary, Digby County, in the Nova Scotia Archives. The woman is reading *Le Petit Courrier*, a French-language weekly that served the Acadian communities throughout Nova Scotia and still publishes to this day. Although this image was taken in 1951, this woman is making her own butter, showing that certain culinary knowledge was still being expressed in the mid-twentieth century. This image was also the background on my computer as I wrote this book, reminding me that daily work is necessary and at times hard, but nourishing nonetheless. NOVA SCOTIA ARCHIVES

ABOUT THIS BOOK AND ITS RECIPES

The point of writing a cookbook is to get people to cook. Each person has their own reason for wanting to cook and own idea of what appeals to them.

For some home cooks, the purpose of cooking is plain and simple: put something on the table that looks good, tastes good, and is easy to make. For others, it's about taking on a little challenge—to learn a new technique or to explore the promise of a new culinary adventure. There are even some who read cookbooks like they read novels: cover to cover, absorbing the information, trying to understand what makes a cuisine taste and work the way it does.

I am all of those people. I'm not every single one of them every day; some days I'm lazy and just want to use up what's in the fridge. That's what the scalloped cabbage dish is for. Some days I feel like I want to practice making potato dumplings and tweak my chicken-stock making, so I make *fricot*. And sometimes, I'm just fascinated by the history of a cuisine, the how-tos and whys. I like to think that all reasons to cook are of equal value and are equally important to transmit.

That's why this book is in your hands.

The recipes in this book come from a variety of sources, and many of them are based on old recipes from my own family and the families of other Acadians. Family lines are the transmission wires for culinary knowledge, and I wanted to pay homage to that. One of the sources of note is a book called *La Cuisine Acadienne d'Aujourd'hui* published in 1963 by Les Dames Patronesses. This book has a special place in the history of southwestern Nova Scotia, as it was used as a fundraiser for the CJA, or Colonie jeunesse acadienne, a camp for Acadian youth. The camp was in operation for decades, and many an Acadian from all over Nova Scotia went there for the summers to have fun in French, their native tongue.

Like most ladies' auxiliary cookbooks, the recipes therein are a time capsule of how people were cooking at a specific time and place. The directions are relatively sparse, as the intended audience—housewives—would need little instruction in comparison to contemporary audiences of amateur cooks and bakers. It even tells something of the fashions of the period, from ingredient and recipe choices—there are copious dessert recipes and a lot of canned- and condensed-milk usage—all the way down to social conventions in how certain recipes are accredited; women are referred to as "Mrs. [insert husband's name]" most of the time. This is why books like these are important: to remind of us of how we ate and how we lived our lives.

Many of the headnotes to these recipes in this book will mention where the recipes come from, whether it's my own family or someone else's.

A lot of these recipes in their original incarnations were nothing more than lists of ingredients. You may not have that culinary base to look at a list of ingredients and know how to proceed. To help everybody out, I've done my best to write out these recipes in clear, descriptive language, telling the home cook what to expect.

The first thing to do when trying out a new recipe is to read it. Don't skim it, looking briefly at the ingredients. Read it once, then read it again. Think back to how many times you claimed to have read a recipe, and then gave up halfway through preparing a dish. Or how many times you declared a recipe a failure because something came up during the cooking process that you didn't understand or expect to happen. Do yourself a favour. Read the recipe, then read it again. Then get everything you need ready, and read it again. Then start cooking. You'll be surprised at how often things work out rather than not.

Sometimes getting your hands dirty is the best way to learn. See page 51 for Salted Green Onions recipe.

PANTRY *and* PALATE

I tried to make things as simple and accessible as possible for all involved when it came down to the ingredients listed in each recipe. An asterisk* will direct the reader to additional information included after the recipe. If the item seems unfamiliar to you, or if you don't have it on hand, check the glossary at the back of the book for information about it.

Not everyone has access to every single ingredient at all times for a multitude of reasons. The recipes in this book will use ingredients that the women and men of a small Acadian community in southwestern Nova Scotia would have had access to during the earlier parts of the twentieth century.

I'd like to thank the testers of these recipes who gave me valuable advice and guidance in knowing what works and what doesn't. I have tried my best to give the novice cook enough information to feel confident when cooking these recipes.

le melangeux dormayex p
farine la poudre a pate et
indoux graduelment en
a vitesse moyenne Jusqua
e consistence ruyeuse 1½

STOCKING YOUR PANTRY

It's important to know what you're going to need when you fill your pantry.
That's what this section is for: to know what to shop for before you begin to
cook these recipes.

Cookbooks and the recipes therein often just list ingredients. And sometimes
home cooks don't know the best ways to buy, store, or use those ingredients.
Some of the best cookbooks out there will go as far as to tell you the brand of the
products that they used and give you options as to what to look for. This can help
you understand and judge the recipes, and it can save you a lot of grief.

The Basics

Although this book is about remembering and reconnecting with ingredients
and flavours of the past, we don't live in the past. Yeast is no longer sold in
cakes; flours are refined and available in all sorts of varieties; and salt can come
in varying sizes, sources, and textures. So to make things easier I've listed these
items, giving you the information you'll need to make sure your dishes turn out
as tasty as possible.

Baking powder. Although you wouldn't think of it as a special ingredient, baking powder has a shelf life: six months to a year once it's been opened, in fact. Write the date on it once you've opened it.

Butter. When it comes to salted or unsalted butter, I leave it up to the discretion of the cook. Trust your own palate. I always use salted when cooking, and often for baking, *but* I know how much salt I need based on the brand I use.

Flour means unbleached white flour. Bleached and enriched white flour will work as well, but I prefer unbleached. If whole wheat flour is required, the recipe will make note. A good rule of thumb is to sub in 1/4 of the amount with whole wheat flour if you want to substitute. You may want to add a little bit more liquid, as the bran in whole wheat tends to absorb more water.

Flour has a shelf life. We don't think of it as having one, but it really does. Especially whole wheat flour. Most commercially available whole-wheat flours start to turn rancid after six months, and if you've been baking with it after that time, you've probably eaten rancid whole wheat. That's probably why you think you don't like the flavour of whole wheat or that you don't like baking with it. Check the dates on the package when you buy it. If you can, buy it in smaller quantities and keep it in a sealed container in the freezer. The taste difference will be noticeable. Unbleached white flours are usually good for about a year.

If you're one of those people who has access to freshly milled flour, you're lucky and should indulge. Here in Atlantic Canada, we have Speerville, a company that produces great flours. Use these as quickly as possible to maintain freshness and see the difference that fresh flour makes. Yes, it costs a bit more, but you'll notice differences in flavour, texture, and even in digestibility. Experiment with flours. Speerville has a great whole wheat flour called Acadia. They also have Red Fife, an heirloom wheat that has been grown in parts of Atlantic Canada and the northeastern states for generations. It has a pleasant nuttiness and lends a slight ruddy colour to bread. If you ever get your hands on a wheat flour called Warthog, snatch it up. I've had the chance to cook with it, and I was able to increase the amount of whole wheat substituted in a recipe from 1/4 to 2/3 without a compromise in flavour. In fact, it enhanced certain breads.

FARMER JOHN'S HERBS

9g

Summer Savory

Natural taste for stuffing, beans, potatoes, eggs, and meat dishes.

Sarriette

Une saveur naturelle pour les farces, les fèves au four, les pommes de terre, les oeufs et les plats de viande.

Product of Nova Scotia · Produit de la Nouvelle-Écosse

www.farmerjohnsherbs.com

Weigh your flour if you can. Kitchen scales are inexpensive, and you'll find yourself more successful when you weigh things. However, if you're measuring flour and you don't have a scale, here's a great tip: use a soup spoon to fluff up the flour, and then spoon it into your measuring cup. You'll get a more accurate reading than if you just dipped and scooped, which can give you way more flour than you think.

Lard is a heavy word, one that has been loaded with negative connotations over the past fifty years due to fat-conscious doctors and diets. It's an ingredient you will often find here in this book. You will even find a recipe for how to render your own lard* (see page 91). Personally, I don't have a problem with using animal-based fats and am somewhat convinced that they could be better for you than vegetable-based shortening, which is hydrogenated so as to be shelf-stable. Feel free to use vegetable-based shortening as a substitute.

Molasses is always fancy-grade. Blackstrap is too intense in flavour. English-style dark treacle is an acceptable substitute.

Salt. I prefer kosher salt, but various brands have different grain sizes. These recipes were created with free-flowing iodized salt, which most people would have access to. If you already are comfortable seasoning with kosher, please do.

Salted Onions/Oignons Salées. People of French descent have been salting herbs and seasonings for centuries—since the time of the Celts. You can occasionally find pre-made salted onions in Acadian community stores, especially in southwestern Nova Scotia (usually next to the bottled clams), but they are ridiculously easy to make. (See recipe on page 51.)

Salt fish can vary in saltiness when purchased. Unlike the European version known as *baccala* (in Italy), *bacalao* (in Spain), or *bacalhao* (in Portugal), which is often sold in large whole and very dry pieces, salt fish in Atlantic Canada often has a higher moisture content, and is sold in plastic bags. The fish was traditionally cod, which keeps its shape quite well when salted; however, many companies in Atlantic Canada will salt other fish such as pollock. Soak the salt fish in cold water overnight and cook up a tiny amount the next morning to taste. You may want to soak it in fresh water at least once more, if not twice.**

Salt pork means salt-cured pork. The three different cuts used to make it are belly, side, and fatback. The most commonly used cuts are fatback and belly. In this book, the recipes will mostly ask for fatback, but feel free to use belly. Bacon is a possible substitute, but the smoke flavour is often overpowering.**

Sugar is granulated white, unless otherwise noted.

Summer Savoury/Sariette. Although not overly common to Acadian pantries in southwestern Nova Scotia, it is a very common herb throughout the rest of the Acadian diaspora, especially in New Brunswick. Thankfully you can purchase it dried in most stores in Atlantic Canada or online through retailers.

Tamarind. Tamarind is the name of a fruit that is native to Africa but used throughout the tropics, from India to Southeast Asia to the Carribbean. The pulp inside the fruit is used as a souring agent in cooking and is often sold semi-dried in packages. Interestingly enough, the term *tamarin* is often used to describe pulled taffy in places like Chéticamp, Nova Scotia, and parts of New Brunswick. You can find it in most Asian grocery stores as well as in specialty grocers.

Yeast. I use active dry yeast when baking. Yes, there are quick-rise yeasts, but they vary from brand to brand, so stick with active dry. The original recipes I consulted asked for yeast cakes, which were way more common during the early part of the twentieth century. Although they are still available—in the refrigerated sections of grocers—I decided to stick with active dry yeast. (For more on yeast and early forms of bread leavening, check out page 63.)

*If you're really interested in animal fats, check out Jennifer McLagan's book *Fat: An Appreciation of a Misunderstood Ingredient, with Recipes*. It's included in the bibliography, and it's thanks to Jennifer that I first learned how to render lard.

**Although not used in this book specifically, I would be remiss if I didn't mention salt pork and salt fish. These two items were commonly found in Acadian pantries and used in many a meal.

1

PRESERVES

Rhubarb pickles done two ways,
recipes start on page 43

THE ART OF CANNING

Putting up. Bottling. Canning. Whatever you want to want to call it, it all comes down to one thing: surviving long winters.

I don't remember where I first heard the expression "endless summer" used to describe the never-ending supply of fruits and vegetables that fill supermarket shelves with produce. Fresh fruits and vegetables that used to have limited and seasonal availability are now available year round. Since the creation of super-markets and refrigerated food distribution over highways, the need to prepare for winter has waned in our collective culinary consciousness.

There is no denying the convenience of no longer being tied by apron strings to a sink full of vegetables and fruits needing to be mixed with salt, sugar, and vine-gar. But like the seasons themselves, things have come full circle, and the cycle of convenience has been broken by an appreciation for seasonality. Ask almost any-one who has a memory of homemade jams, pickles, and preserves, and they will probably tell you that those homemade items were much better than what is on the shelves of their local supermarket (and probably their own kitchen shelves).

Canning and bottling as necessities are no longer paramount to our homes, but there is something lost when the craft and knowledge of such foods is left to large-scale producers. There are few joys in this world like that which comes from feeding oneself from foodstuffs one had the foresight and know-how to make, let alone sharing that food with others.

I'm lucky enough to have grown up in a household where many pickles and pre-serves were made. I'll admit to a predilection for the memories that present them-selves when opening canned fruit that was made during an afternoon of peeling, seasoning, and boiling. There is nostalgia for that moment: the season that has now passed, in recent memory or in childhood. Author Marcel Proust may have waxed poetic about beautiful madeleine cookies in a Parisian parlour, but for me, the snap of a jar being opened and the jewelled colours of preserves lining a pan-try cupboard are much more evocative.

Canning and bottling doesn't have to be scary. There are innumerable books and websites that can teach you how to do it at home safely and efficiently. A great book on the subject is Andrea Weigl's *Pickles & Preserves*. Weigl is a food writer for the *News & Observer* in Raleigh, North Carolina. She is, in her own words, "a northerner by birth and a southerner by circumstance." Although she lives and cooks in the American South and makes use of the ingredients grown thereabout, her book has sage advice for any amateur or first-timer when it comes to putting up for the winter. "My year is defined by canning sessions," she writes. I've been lucky enough to sample some of the fruits that were put up during those sessions, and they are quite magical. I asked her for permission to use some of the advice offered in her book, which is both quoted and paraphrased here.

Once you've tried putting up fruits and vegetables in jars, you'll realize how relatively easy it can be. At its most basic, you will need:

1. a large pot for boiling and sealing your jars (make sure that there is enough room for the jars as well as a couple inches of water to properly cover them);
2. clean jars and new lids;
3. a wide-mouth canning funnel;
4. a jar lifter;
5. a rack that will fit inside your pot;
6. clean kitchen towels; and
7. a rack to let the bottles cool.

You can find all of these items in grocery and hardware stores, and they aren't prohibitively expensive. You may be surprised at how often you end up using any and all of these items, not just for canning.

I find the most efficient thing is to have your foodstuffs ready to be canned (either cooked already or ready to be cooked by a hot bath), your jars and lids washed and rinsed, and your pot full of boiling water.

The first thing to do is to make sure everything is clean and sanitized. Wash your jars in warm soapy water and then rinse and dry them with a clean towel. Keep a small pot on the stove filled with water and new clean lids and tops for the bottles. Bring the water to just below a gentle simmer to help moisten the rubber ring and keep things warm. "The lids must be heated for at least 10 minutes to achieve a vacuum seal," says Weigl. Place your rack on the bottom of the large pot. If you don't have an extra rack, a thick kitchen towel on the bottom will do the trick.

Weigl suggests placing the cleaned and empty jars into your large pot full of boiling water. I follow my mother's example of putting the cleaned jars into a warm oven to sit and wait for filling. In any scenario, carefully remove the hot jars from whererever they are onto the countertop. Using your funnel, fill the jars, making sure to leave a little room at the top. Many Mason jars will have a slight indentation where they curve upwards, giving you a bit of a guide as to where to stop. You want to avoid having any bubbles in your jar, so if whatever you're preserving is thick (think of jams), Weigl says to use "a thin plastic spatula to slowly stir the contents of each jar to release any air bubbles and run the spatula around the inside of the jar, which will make sure the jar seals properly."

Use a clean damp cloth to wipe any excess food from the rim of the jars. Remove the lids from their water bath and place on each jar. Place the screw bands on top and turn until nice and tight. Place the jars into the water gently, making sure to give each jar enough room in the pot.

For the recipes in this chapter, cooking times are listed in the individual recipes, as they tend to vary.

Remove the jars using your jar lifter—seriously, get one, I've burned myself on hot water too many times to count—and place them on a rack or towel-lined counter. Soon enough you'll hear a distinctive popping sound—that's the lids sealing. Don't touch the lids until you hear this sound: if they pop due to the pressure of being touched, they may not have sealed properly. Weigl recommends leaving them undisturbed for 12 to 24 hours and then checking to make sure the lids are properly sealed: "Each lid should be concave and shouldn't move when pressed with a finger."

Canned goods made in this manner tend to have a shelf life of about a year if stored in a dark area. Once opened, they should be used within a month, says Weigl. (You can find out more about Weigl in the Bibliography on page 237.)

Candy-cane, or Chioggia, beet
ready to be pickled

Pickled Beets.

Cook beets as usual.
For eight medium sized
beets prepare three eighths

PICKLED BEETS MAKES 2 (500ML) JARS

"Cook beets as usual," the instructions say.

I'm not 100 per cent sure what "as usual" meant for my grandmother Rosalie. It probably meant boiled and served with a side of stained hands, counters, and wooden spoons. I remember my own mother, her hands stained deep pink with beet juice.

My parents didn't have to pickle anything. They just chose to. Looking back, my parents did a lot of things they didn't have to. But together they filled their cold storage with jars, lining the shelves with pickled and canned goods. I like to think that my parents, Jeanne and Hector, had a respect for the work that produced such a larder.

Late summer and early fall weekends meant work for my parents. Standing over a large pot, billows of vinegared steam filling the air, to- gether they chopped and peeled. My father sat hunched over in a chair, his scraps going into a bin. I was envious of his deftness with a small paring knife. I still am. Jeanne would be the one making the brine. She knew how much sugar and vinegar was needed. She'd occasionally double-check her measurements by consulting an old recipe, but soon enough muscle and taste memory came into play.

It wasn't until I was in my late thirties that I understood what they were doing. Years of marriage, companionship, conversation, and a mutual respect and understanding made these two sit down and work. Because by working together, they fed our family. They fed our memories.

In my own kitchen I stand in front of what looks like a pound of scrubbed and trimmed beets. I've learned that I can avoid the stained hands if I use Chioggia, also known as candy-cane beets, which also add a nice visual dimension to a classic. A large pot of water is waiting to boil. A smaller one behind it is filled with a vinegar, water, and sugar solution that is lying in wait. Soon the two will meet in a few canning jars. Some will go straight to the fridge, and others will be given a hot bath to save them for the long winter. I only want a small amount. That's my usual. That's what I need.

Note: This recipe is for a small amount but can easily be doubled or tripled. Although most pickled beet recipes ask for copious amounts of salt, this recipe did not, and is sweeter than most. I added a teaspoon of salt, just to liven it up.

3/4 pound beets, scrubbed, tops removed
1 teaspoon salt
3/4 cup sugar
1 1/2 cups water
3/4 cup white vinegar

- First you want to ensure that all of your beets have been cut into roughly the same size so they will cook evenly. Think about the size you would want when you pick them out of their jar. That's a good place to start.

- Place beets and salt in a large pot and bring to a boil. Cook for about 15–20 minutes, depending on the size of beets. They're done when just about fork-tender.

- Once cooked, strain and place beets into sterile Mason jars. Leave enough room to cover with pickling liquid and leave 1/4-inch headspace.

- Meanwhile, in a saucepan over medium heat, add sugar, water, and vinegar. Stir to dissolve sugar.

- Bring to a roiling boil for about 2–3 minutes. You want this liquid to be as hot as possible for pouring into your jars.

- Pour boiling liquid into jars, covering beets completely, and leave 1/4 inch of headspace.

- Cover jars with lids, and either place in fridge to eat within a few weeks or can as you normally would*, boiling the jars in a hot-water bath for 15–20 minutes.

*Canning "as you normally would" is covered starting on page 33.

Cider Brine for Beets

This slight variation for brine is a little more spiced and flavourful. Follow the steps for making the brine as listed on the previous page. You can also play with the flavouring by using cloves, allspice berries, or even star anise. That last one may not be traditional, but it is still quite tasty.

3/4 cup sugar
1 1/2 cups water
1/2 cup cider vinegar
1/4 cup white vinegar
1 star anise, 2–3 cloves, 2–3 spice berries, in any combination (optional)

➤ Over medium heat, bring the sugar, water, any seasonings you may be using, cider vinegar, and white vinegar to a boil.

➤ Use as in previous recipe or, to allow the seasonings to shine even more, allow the brine to cool overnight in the fridge. Strain the seasonings from the brine, and then return to a boil for canning.

PICKLED RHUBARB (DONE TWO WAYS)

I adore rhubarb: rhubarb jam, rhubarb chutney, rhubarb steeped in teas and tisanes, rhubarb in custard pies (see page 199), rhubarb in pies with strawberry, rhubarb made into cordials—the list goes on and on. When rhubarb stalks are very thin and very pink I nibble on them dipped into sugar. I find great joy in discovering new recipes for what to do with rhubarb, and so I was just as happy to find a few recipes in my family notebooks.

Some people are leery of rhubarb. It is actually a vegetable, not a fruit, so people can feel a little deceived by it. Then there is the issue of the leaves, which are very high in oxalic acid and can have a less than pleasant digestive effect. The plant itself also has a tendency to sprawl, so gardeners often swear at it rather than by it. I don't. I pester the farmers at the market as soon as spring hits, waiting to see it piled on the tables for sale.

I found this recipe for pickled rhubarb, which in its original form is very much like chutney. It also asked for a lot more sugar and used pure white vinegar. I reduced the amount of sugar and subbed in equal amounts of white and cider vinegar. The original recipe asked for all of the ingredients to be cooked together for half an hour. However, I find that a lot of people aren't into either cooking or eating rhubarb because of how it goes from perfectly cooked to falling apart in a matter of minutes, so texture was an issue. But after having eaten pickled rhubarb as part of a wonderful dish in a restaurant, I realized I could have both textures by cooking half of the rhubarb and then adding more of it at the end with the stove turned off, thereby cooking with the residual heat.

The second version of the recipe I have listed here uses this same idea—residual heat to cook the rhubarb—but this time, the residual heat is from the boiling-vinegar bath that goes over the rhubarb when it is already in the Mason jar for canning. Serve it as you would a cranberry sauce. It goes very well with cured meats.

Tip: When cooking with rhubarb, try and find stalks of equal thickness, especially when you want the pieces to stay whole. It leads to more consistent cooking times and texture.

VERSION 1 **THE CHUTNEY** MAKES 2 (500ML) JARS

1 1/2 pounds rhubarb
1 cup white vinegar
1 cup cider vinegar
1 teaspoon salt
1 1/2 cups sugar
1 tablespoon fresh ground ginger
1 teaspoon cinnamon, or 1 (1/2-inch) cinnamon stick
1 teaspoon ground cloves
1 small onion, cut into rings

- Wash rhubarb in a sink full of cold water. Make sure to cut off any leafy ends, which is where most oxalic acid is located. Cut into 1/2-inch pieces.

- In a pot large enough to accommodate all of your ingredients, add vinegars, spices, salt, and sugar and place over medium heat. Bring to

a gentle simmer and then add onion. Cook for about 5 minutes, or just enough to soften the onions.

- Add 1 pound of rhubarb to the pot, reserving remaining 1/2 pound, and cover the pot. Cook for 10 minutes until rhubarb has broken apart.

- Turn the heat off and add remaining rhubarb. Cover the pot for 5 minutes and then pour the chutney into a jar or bowl. Chill until ready to serve.

- If you want to can this preserve, follow the instructions for canning on page 33.

VERSION 2 PICKLED PIECES MAKES 2 (500ML) JARS

1 pound rhubarb
1 small onion, sliced thinly into rings
2 cups white vinegar, or 1 cup white vinegar and 1 cup cider vinegar
1 1/2 cups sugar
1 teaspoon ground cinnamon, or 1 (1/2-inch) cinnamon stick
1 teaspoon whole allspice berries
1 teaspoon salt

- Wash rhubarb in a sink full of cold water. Make sure to cut off any leafy ends, which is where most of the oxalic acid is located. Cut into 1/2-inch pieces and place into a glass jar or another container that can be sealed. Add onion slices.

- Add vinegar, spices, salt, and sugar to a pot and place over medium heat. Bring to a gentle simmer and stir until the sugars have dissolved.

- Increase heat to bring the liquid to a boil. Keep it at this heat for about 1 minute.

- Turn heat off and pour boiling liquid over rhubarb and onion.

- If you want to can this preserve, follow the instructions for canning on page 33. If eating within 1 week, simply close the container and cool in the fridge.

MUSTARD PICKLES MAKES 4 (500ML) JARS

The one thing I found the most interesting in the original recipe for
Mustard Pickles from Tante Lalie's notebook was the inclusion of tomatoes. I have to say I omitted them, but if you feel so inclined, add 4 cups of
tomatoes. I would use green tomatoes for a firmer texture, but I made this
without tomatoes and it was lovely. The recipe also asks for ground mustard, but feel free to add a few extra mustard seeds to each jar as you place
the pickle inside.

4 cups cucumbers, cut into slices
4 cups cauliflower, cut into small florets
4 cups onions, sliced finely
1 cup salt
1 gallon ice

1 cup flour
1 cup sugar
1 tablespoon ground mustard
8 cups vinegar (preferably cider, or a blend of cider and white)

- Place vegetables in a large container, preferably glass or plastic. Cover with ice and add the salt. Leave them to sit overnight.

- Strain vegetables and rinse with cold water. Give them a taste. If they're still too salty, give them another good rinse.

- Prep your jars for canning. (See The Art Of Canning on page 33.)

- In a large pot, combine sugar, flour, and mustard and mix thoroughly. Cup by cup add the vinegar to create a paste. Cook paste over medium-low heat, stirring to prevent scorching, for about 5–6 minutes, to help eliminate the taste of raw flour.

- Add the vegetables and enough water to cover. Bring to a simmer, cooking for roughly 8–10 minutes.

- Ladle the vegetable and vinegar mixture into your jars, leaving a good 1/4-inch headspace. Make sure to clean the edges before placing the lids on.

- Place the jars in a hot-water bath for 10 minutes. Remove and allow to rest.

OIGNONS SALÉES / SALTED GREEN ONIONS

I first wrote the recipe for salted onions in a piece I did for *East Coast Living* magazine a few years ago. The story was about the preservation of old recipes and culinary techniques, and in it I wrote about this indispensable condiment to Acadians from southwestern Nova Scotia.

Salting is one of the oldest preservation methods known to man, and for generations it was essential to any Acadian pantry. Although the salting of meats and vegetables is no longer necessary in contemporary kitchens, the flavour that comes from salted foods is hard to replace.

Salted green onions (scallions) are a good example. Found throughout southwestern Nova Scotia and in many other Acadian communities, the briny onion kick provided by this pantry staple is often the base note in foods such as rappie pie, fricot, *and many more recipes. Although you could simply substitute salt and fresh onions when cooking, the alchemy that is created when these two ingredients are left to their own devices to merge together is unforgettable and nearly irreplaceable.*

The practice of salting green onions/scallions—as well as other herbs—is also known throughout most of French-speaking Canada. In parts of New Brunswick and way into rural Québec, salted herbs such as summer savoury, wild thyme, and various other wild plants were used as a way of keeping dishes fresh and bright-tasting, especially when greenery was in short supply during long winters.

There is no real "recipe" for making this condiment because everyone just made it in their homes. You add salt to chopped green onions. That's pretty much it. When I asked my father for any tips or advice, he simply said, "When you think you've got enough salt, keep adding it." He followed that up by saying that's how his father taught him: "You can never have too much salt, but you can definitely not have enough."

The recipe for this is therefore painfully simple, but that's also what makes it somewhat opaque. Some people prefer to make a heavy brine (the ratio varies from house to house, but usually there is "enough salt in the water to make a potato float," as the old wives' tale goes), but I prefer to place the green onions in coarse salt and pack them tightly into a Mason jar.

You need salt, preferably kosher or a large-grained salt, Mason jars (or any reasonable jar that will close and seal properly), and green onions. Loads of them. If you have green onions in your backyard garden that have gone a little high and are sturdy from trying to go to seed, even better.

green onions (scallions)
large-grained salt/kosher salt

- Start by chopping off the roots of your green onions. Roughly chop green onions from base to tip and place them in a large glass or plastic bowl. Add enough salt so that green onions look like they are covered in small crystals. Mix them together. And then add the same amount of salt as you did the first time. Mix it all together again, and then let it sit overnight, preferably in a cool place.

- The next day you'll notice the volume of green onions has decreased slightly and you may have a bit of brine in the bottom. What you want to do is add more salt (crazy, I know), until green onions look somewhat like they did when you first added salt. Think about it. You're trying to inhibit any microbacterial activity for a year. That's a lot of salt. "*Sale à la vielle façon*," said my dad. "Salt it in the old way."

- Pack green onions tightly into Mason jars and close the lid. They will last for up to a year. If you want them to keep their colour, feel free to place them in the freezer. Use in soups, stews, dumplings, rappie pies, *fricot*, or anywhere else you need a salty and oniony kick. A little goes a long way.

(Tamarin)

½ livre de tamarin

2 tasse d'eau chaude

brasser le jusqu'au temps qu'il soit défai...

2 tasse de Sucre

¾ " " " Mélasse

½

TAMARIND SPREAD   MAKES ROUGHLY 1 LITRE

"Taste this," I said as I passed the tiny brown pastille to my mother. I had been at an Asian grocer the day before and had filled a candy bowl with individually wrapped tamarind candies from Thailand.

You could tell a memory was forming somewhere in her head, and she was trying to locate it. "Tastes like something I had in my childhood," she said. Why would a woman who grew up in 1950s Atlantic Canada have a childhood memory filled with such a tropical flavour?

The answer is steeped in history and economics.

For along time, the waters that surround Atlantic Canada were known for their prodigious quantities of fish. Much of the fish caught was cod and haddock, and much of that was salted for later consumption. That fish was also traded as a commodity down in *les îles*, the Carribean Islands. This is part of the history of much of the region.

Tamarind came to the Caribbean islands through the slave trade as well as through workers from South Asia, who brought the fruit with them and used it as a souring agent in cooking. Sweet varieties of the fresh fruit's pulp were also consumed occasionally as a snack.

We know that molasses came from the islands (see Molasses Cake on page 173), as well as rum and whole spices, but traders also brought back tamarind. Unlike citrus fruits, which were somewhat expensive and had short shelf lives, tamarind pulp has a long shelf life and contains as much (if not more) vitamin C. Many Acadians would add boiling water to tamarind pulp, as well as sugar and/or molasses, and slather the spread on toast.

In his book, *Whispers of the Past*, amateur historian and *raconteur* Edward S. d'Entremont talks about the general store his family owned and operated in Lower East Pubnico, an Acadian village in Yarmouth County, Nova Scotia. He mentions tamarind as one of the many foodstuffs brought up from the West Indies. "Molasses came in puncheons [very large barrels].... Tamarinds were very much in vogue as 'something to dip your spoon into' like the older generation would say."

Today, tamarind is most often found in South Asian and Southeast Asian grocery stores, but believe it or not, you can even find it in grocery stores in my hometown of Church Point, Nova Scotia. According to the store owners, the majority of its consumers are people over the age of seventy who still look for a taste of the old days.

Interestingly enough, the name *tamarin* also refers to a brown sugar or molasses-based taffy candy that is eaten in Acadian communities in Cape Breton. But in this case, we're sticking to the stuff that came up from the Carribbean, via South Asia, into the pantries of many Acadians.

1 block tamarind pulp, roughly 400 grams
3 1/2 cups water
2 cups sugar
3/4 cup molasses

- Place tamarind in a large bowl, breaking it up into pieces.
- Bring 3 cups of water to a vigorous boil.
- Pour boiling water over tamarind pulp. Break up any larger pieces and cover with cling film for about 30 minutes.
- Strain through a fine-meshed sieve, pushing to remove as much liquid as possible. Throw away any seeds or leftover pulp.
- In a large saucepan, bring sugar, molasses, and remaining 1/2 cup of water to a gentle simmer.
- Mix molasses mixture into tamarind liquid. Allow to cool and pour into individual containers or jars.*
- Serve on fresh or toasted bread as a jam/jelly.

*At this point you could can your tamarind. For more information on canning, see page 33.

2 BREADS

HOPS, POTATOES, FLOUR, YEAST

It's important to remember that for thousands of years, bread truly was the staff of life for people. It was the cornerstone of the table, a filling and nutritious form of sustenance. Historically speaking, white bread was a sign of luxury. It meant you could afford to have pure white flour freed from its bran (which went rancid quickly). The lack of bran gave the flour a longer shelf life. Interestingly enough, according to Marielle Cormier-Boudreau and Melvin Gallant's *A Taste of Acadie*, white bread was a staple for the Acadians, at least until the Deportation. After that, "the wheat harvest was generally poor on the land on which they were forced to live, and white flour was a commodity they could rarely afford." That's putting it mildly. The land that many Acadian families worked after the Deportation was not the best for growing wheat, but thankfully buckwheat grew relatively well. Breads of all kinds were eaten in many Acadian homes in various forms. Today packaged white bread is no longer seen as a luxury item that liberated women from the drudgery of baking daily, but rather as a bland, tasteless filler.

Until the popularity of cake yeast (and later dry instant yeast, which is found in most people's pantries today), breads were leavened by various methods: either through fermenting part of a bread dough to create a *levain*, leaven as it is known in English, or by boiling hops and potatoes and fermenting the mash left over from the two. The method for making such a mash, like all good recipes, depends on whom you ask.

In the book *Cuisine de Cheticamp*, Ginette Aucoin mentions that baking bread "could take as long as 2 days." Aucoin talks about using "ups," which were also used for making beer. Although the French word for them is *houblon*, Aucoin is indeed talking about hops, which would have been pronounced "ups" by the French-speaking Acadians of the region. In *Travel On*, Jean Doris LeBlanc, another Acadian from Cape Breton, writes that hops would be placed into a canvas bag, which was then placed in a pot of boiling water and potatoes. "The mixture is boiled for about an hour—until the water turns colour. We then take out the bag of hops and put it away to be used another time. We can generally use it twice before it's worn out. After this we pick out the potatoes, one at a time, with a large spoon and mash them in the spoon with a fork, then drop the mashed material back into the liquid. When all the potatoes are mashed, we pour the thick liquid into a crock and cork it. It can be used immediately."

In this section of the book, I won't be asking you to do anything that involved, but learning how to bake bread has made me appreciate the eating of bread tenfold. For Acadians, meals often began with bread and butter—and molasses— and often ended on the very same note. Once you make these breads, you'll know why.

(Left) Acadian camp cook from
Saulnierville Station, Nova Scotia, baking
bread at mid-morning, August 1950.
NOVA SCOTIA ARCHIVES

BRAN BREAD   MAKES 1 LOAF

If you were to go back in time—a little over one hundred years—you would easily find small community mills in most rural areas. Grist- and flour mills would mill the grains that many people grew for their own flour. Grains such as oats, various types of summer and winter wheat, buckwheat, and flax were grown for food and as cover and rotation crops. Because of the volatile oils in the bran, the flour would have a shorter shelf life than what we buy today. In later years, some mills came to have the capacity to separate the bran from the flour, but that nutritious bran was still desired, and eaten.

In France, *pain au son*, or bran bread, has to be at least 20 per cent bran by law. This particular bran bread is a little dense, and it is flavoured with raisins, which can be omitted easily if putting raisins in your bread isn't your thing.

In figuring out this recipe, I found myself making a simple porridge with hot water and the bran, and then adding moisture and sweetness in the form of molasses. The freshness of your bran and how long you allow it to soak in the liquid will affect the density of the bread. It's also worth noting that this bread gains its lift from baking soda rather than yeast. The original handwritten recipe for this bread asks for milk that may be "sour or sweet," so feel free to use whole milk or buttermilk, depending on what you have in your fridge.

1 cup (scant) wheat bran or oat bran
1 heaping cup flour
1 teaspon baking soda
pinch of salt
1/2 cup molasses
1 cup milk
1/4 cup raisins (optional)
1 cup water

- Preheat oven to 400°F. Grease and flour a loaf pan.

- Bring 1 cup of water to a gentle simmer. Pour over bran and allow to cool, about 40 minutes.

- Sift flour with soda and salt.

- Add molasses to bran porridge. Mix well.

- Add flour to the mixture and mix well, making sure that all flour is moistened.

- Add milk (and raisins, if using) and stir until batter is thickened and all ingredients are well blended.

- Pour into the loaf pan and place in the oven. Bake for 45 minutes.

CORNMEAL AND MOLASSES SANDWICH BREAD

The first time I tried making this bread, I knew it would be perfect for people who have never baked bread or who have been intimidated by the process. This is a very sturdy dough that can handle heavy kneading and a good amount of flour; it teaches a baker to understand one of the most important things you can learn in making bread: the feel of the dough.

I found versions of this recipe in multiple books, both private and published. One version came from a small blue notebook that was owned by my grandfather Augustin's cousin Denis. The notebook looked like it was cobbled together from various family sources, with hints, tips, and recipes for the batchelor. I found the same recipe, written verbatim, in another notebook by Rosalie, Augustin's wife. It is a popular recipe that has been transmitted from one generation to the next.

What is interesting about this bread is that it's a prime example of a food found throughout Atlantic Canada. I found a version of it in a book of recipes written by descendants of Black Loyalists who brought the use of cornmeal in breads with them from the United States in the 1800s. This makes sense, since cornmeal is found in many a Loyalist pantry and also in many an African American pantry throughout the American South. The bread is also known as Anadama bread in Boston. Its colourful name comes from the rather apocryphal tale of a man who was tired of eating the same cornmeal mush his wife served him every day. "Anna, damn her," he apparently said, and added yeast, flour, and molasses to his mush and baked it into a bread.

It doesn't matter who came up with this bread or who cooked it first. What matters is that it was shared and eaten because it's delicious.

CORNMEAL AND MOLASSES SANDWICH BREAD
MAKES 2 LOAVES

Breads made with grain porridges like the one used in this recipe are a great way to add fibre or bulk to bread, especially in places (or times) where refined flour would be scarce. The amount of flour required here is a little more open-ended than other recipes because of a few variables in making this bread. Depending on how long the cornmeal is left to absorb the water, you will need more or less flour for kneading. If you've never kneaded dough before, it's a pretty simple process, one which you will get the hang of faster than you think. Trust the dough, it will "tell" you how much flour it needs when you knead it. The nice thing with this dough is that you don't have to be gentle with it, so don't worry about over-kneading it. Find a video online for hints, or even better, ask a friend to show you how to knead. A dough scraper can also help you pick up all the loose bits of bread dough off of your counter and aid in cleanup.

This is a great everyday bread that can be eaten on its own, used for sand-wiches, or toasted.

3/4 cup cornmeal, plus 1 tablespoon for dusting
2 teaspoons sugar
3 teaspoons lard (or vegetable shortening)
2 cups boiling water

1/3 cup room temperature water
2 teaspoons yeast
1 teaspoon baking soda
2 teaspoons salt
1/2 cup molasses
4–5 cups flour, plus 1 tablespoon for dusting

➤ In a bowl, mix cornmeal, sugar, and lard. Add the boiling water and mix thoroughly to eliminate any lumps. Let cool for about 45 minutes.

The cornmeal will expand and look somewhat like porridge. Just make sure that the porridge is cool enough for the yeast to become active, rather than too hot, which can kill the yeast.

- In room-temperature water, thoroughly mix the yeast and baking soda. Add this to your cornmeal porridge, then add salt and molasses. Mix until well blended.

- Stir in flour 1 cup at a time, making sure flour is completely incorporated before you add more. By the time you have finished incorporating the third cup of flour, the dough should start to come together, pulling away from the sides of the bowl. Turn the dough out onto a floured surface, and dust it with more flour to start kneading.

- With flour-dusted hands, gather the dough into a large ball and begin to knead the dough. The dough will be slightly tacky at first; a good rule of thumb for this bread is to keep adding small amounts of flour as you knead it. Eventually the dough will become rather smooth and no longer tacky, and it will feel taut and less elastic as you knead it.

- Place the dough in a clean bowl, cover it with cling film, and allow it to rest for about 45 minutes. Take the dough out and knead it gently for about 1 minute. It will feel very elastic compared to your previous kneading. Place back in bowl and allow it to rise for about 1 hour.

- Grease your pans with a little lard, and dust with 1 tablespoon flour and 1 tablespoon cornmeal. Take the dough out of its bowl, and cut it in half. These will be your two loaves. Gently pinch the ends of the dough to shape the loaves. Place each loaf in a greased and floured loaf pan. Allow to rise for another hour.

- Preheat your oven to 400°F. Place the bread into the oven and bake for 1 hour.

- Remove the bread from the oven and remove the loaves from the pans. They should fall out quite easily. The bread should sound hollow when tapped on the bottom. If not, return to oven for 10 minutes, without the loaf pan.

- Allow the bread to cool for at least 1 hour before cutting into it.

Corn Meal Bread. (2 loaves

¼ cup corn meal
2 cups boiling water
2 teaspoons sugar
teaspoons lard. Let cool. Then

VERSION 2 CORNMEAL SANDWICH BREAD MAKES 2 LOAVES

Although I am a big fan of the previous bread recipe for Cornmeal and
Molasses Sandwich Bread, sometimes I run out of molasses. This happened
one day when I was testing the other recipe for the umpteenth time. I
imagine that in times of want, there would have been an Acadian cook who
would've found themselves without molasses. I've also omitted the baking
soda and the lard. It will rise slower than the previous recipe due to the
lack of sugar (molasses) for the yeast to feed on. This bread doesn't have as
long a shelf life as its progenitor, but it's so tasty on its own—especially as
toast—that I doubt your loaves will go stale.

3/4 cup cornmeal, plus 1 tablespoon for dusting
1 tablespoon honey
2 teaspoons salt
2 cups boiling water
1/3 cup room temperature water
2 teaspoons yeast
4–5 cups flour, plus 1 tablespoon for dusting

- In a bowl, mix cornmeal, honey, and salt. Add boiling water and mix thoroughly. Let cool for about 45 minutes. The cornmeal will expand and look somewhat like porridge.

- In room-temperature water, add yeast. Mix until well blended. Add to porridge.

- Stir in flour 1 cup at a time, making sure the flour is completely incorporated before you add more. By the time you have finished incorporating the third cup of flour, the dough should start to come together, pulling away from the sides. Turn the dough out onto a well-floured surface, and dust it with more flour to start kneading.

- With flour-dusted hands, gather the dough into a large ball and begin to knead the dough. The dough will be slightly tacky at first; a good rule of thumb for this bread is to keep adding small amounts of flour as you knead it. Eventually the dough will become rather smooth and no longer tacky, and it will feel taut and less elastic as you knead it.

- Place the dough in a clean bowl and allow it to rest for about 45 minutes. Take the dough out and knead it gently for about 1 minute. It will feel very elastic compared to your previous kneading. Place back in bowl and allow it to rise for about 1 hour.

- Grease your pans with a little lard, and dust with 1 tablespoon flour and 1 tablespoon cornmeal. Take the dough out of its bowl, and cut it in half. These will be your two loaves. Gently pinch the ends of the dough to shape the loaves. Place each loaf in a greased and floured loaf pan. Allow to rise for another hour.

- Preheat your oven to 400°F. Place the bread into the oven and bake for 1 hour.

- Remove the bread from the oven and remove the loaves from the pans. They should fall out quite easily. The bread should sound hollow when tapped on the bottom. If not, return to oven for 10 minutes, without the loaf pan.

- Allow the bread to cool for at least an hour before cutting into it.

JOHNNY CAKES MAKES 6–10 CAKES, DEPENDING ON SIZE

How johnny cakes came to be part of Acadian kitchens throughout the Maritimes speaks to the influence of the many Loyalists who fled the United States and came to Canada in the mid-1800s. They brought with them various cooking habits and ingredients from throughout the eastern American seaboard, including all the way from the Carolinas. This cornmeal bread has been eaten, cooked, and made in many ways over the years. It is an example of how culinary cultures can intermingle.

In his 1978 book, *Waste Not, Want Not: A Book of Cookery*, E. F. "Ted" Eaton provides a recipe that is more of a dessert, and he uses quite a bit of maple syrup. Instead of a belly-filling staple that was eaten along with meals, Eaton states that "johnnycake—or more properly, journey-cake—is a very old dessert and was a great favourite in New England well before the American Revolution. [...] This recipe is capable of infinite variations in texture and flavour by varying the proportion of maple syrup to milk."

In her 1983 book, *Loyalist Foods in Today's Recipes*, author Eleanor Robert Smith lists them as "corn pones," and prefaces her recipe by saying, "Indian meal (cornmeal) was a staple of the Loyalists. Hot corn breads went by various names such as johnny cakes, hoe cakes and corn pones." She also suggests that if you have the chance to make them over an open fire, to do so on a greased hoe.

To me, cornbreads like this have always been distinctively southern and very much part of the foods that would've been cooked by people of African American descent in the southern United States. Recently, there has been a lot of discussion about the whitewashing of southern food and the reclamation of that heritage by authors like Toni Tipton Martin (*The Jemima Code*) and Michael W. Twitty (*The Cooking Gene*).

This recipe comes from Tante Lalie's notebook, and it probably dates from the early 1900s. Eat these johnny cakes with baked beans, as a snack with butter and molasses, or as an accompaniment to any meal.

2 cups white flour
2 teaspoons cream of tartar
1 teaspoon baking soda
1/2 teaspoon salt
4 cups cornmeal
1/4 cup melted lard or vegetable oil
3 eggs
1 cup milk

- Sift together flour, cream of tartar, baking soda, and salt.

- Add cornmeal and stir until well incorporated.

- Preheat a skillet or griddle to medium/medium-high. Add a small portion of lard or vegetable oil to just grease the surface.

- In a separate bowl, mix eggs and milk together.

- Add the liquid to the dry ingredients and whisk together until there are no clumps.

- Pour a small amount of batter into the skillet, about the size of the palm of your hand. Just like you would with regular pancakes, make sure not to overpour, lest you overcrowd the pan with too many johnny cakes. Cook until bubbles appear on the surface of the batter and then flip. Serve immediately.

OAT BREAD MAKES 1 LOAF

Porridge-based breads are some of the easiest and most nutritious to make, since the scalding of the grain allows the bread to soften and makes it easier to digest. This recipe for an oat-based porridge bread was one I found in Lalie's notebooks and was one of the few that actually included instructions, rather than just a list of ingredients. I also found a very similar version in the *Les Dames Patronesses* cookbook—a version written by Mrs. Edith Tufts. Edith was a historian, an archivist, and a stauch promotor of Acadian heritage. She even went on to create a colouring book for Acadian children, all the way back in 1978. Mrs. Tufts surely would have made this bread many times in her life, especially since she had seventeen children to feed.

This recipe was very familiar to me, as I had been baking an oat bran bread in my own kitchen for quite some time. This type of bread made me very comfortable with the act baking bread by helping me to understand the variations that can occur in bread making. Armed with that base knowledge—both in my hands and in my head—this bread was an easy one to make. Like the cornmeal molasses bread, this recipe is great for beginners.

2 cups water
1 cup oats
2 tablespoons sugar
1 tablespoon salt
1/2 cup molasses
2 teaspoons yeast
5 1/2–6 cups flour

- Bring 1 cup of water just to a gentle boil.
- Add the oats to a large bowl. Scald the oats with the boiling water, and allow to cool slightly, about 20–30 minutes.
- In another bowl, use 1/2 cup of room temperature water and dissolve the sugar, salt, and molasses.
- Dissolve the yeast in the remaining 1/2 cup of water (at room temperature).
- Add the yeast water along with the molasses water to the oat porridge.
- Add the flour, 1 cup at a time, stirring to incorporate completely before adding more. The bread is ready to be kneaded once the dough has come away from the sides of the bowl.
- With flour-dusted hands, gather the dough into a large ball and begin to knead the dough. The dough will be slightly tacky at first; a good rule of thumb for this bread is to keep adding small amounts of flour as you knead it. Eventually the dough will become rather smooth and no longer tacky, and it will feel taut and less elastic as you knead it.
- Place the dough in a clean bowl, cover it with cling film, and allow it to rest for about 45 minutes. Take the dough out and knead it gently for about 1 minute. It will feel very elastic compared to your previous kneading. Place back in the bowl, cover, and allow the dough to rise for about 1 hour.
- Take the dough out and cut in half for two loaves. Gently pinch the ends of the dough to shape the loaves. Place each loaf in a greased and floured loaf pan. Allow to rise for another hour.
- Preheat your oven to 400°F. Place the bread into the oven and bake for 1 hour.
- Remove the bread from the oven and remove from pans. The bread should sound hollow when tapped on the bottom. If not, return the loaf, without the pan, to the oven for 10 minutes.
- Allow the bread to cool for at least 1 hour before cutting into it.

WHITE BREAD (DONE TWO WAYS)

In Rosalie and Eulalie's notebooks, there are multiple recipes for bread. But the two that intrigued me the most were for what seemed like a "special" white bread, and a utilitarian white bread recipe.

VARIATION 1 WORKHORSE WHITE BREAD MAKES 2 LOAVES

I called this recipe "Workhorse White Bread" because it is simple in its making, is low maintenance, but isn't afraid of a little hard work. This is bread dough that you can smack, slap, slam, and punch. This bread recipe was made for large families that ate bread with every meal. Thankfully, you can also freeze this bread quite easily, either whole or presliced.

2 teaspoons yeast
3 1/2 cups water, room temperature
1 tablespoon sugar
1 teaspoon salt
2 tablespoons lard or shortening
6–7 cups flour

- Dissolve the yeast in the water. Add the sugar, salt, and lard/shortening.

- One cup at a time, add flour, making sure to incorporate as much as possible before adding more.

- After about 4 or 5 cups, when the dough begins to take shape and loosen itself from the sides of the bowl, place dough on a well-floured surface to knead.

- Keep adding flour while kneading. You don't have to be gentle with this dough. Feel free to drop it from high above the counter, stretch it, or take out your frustrations on it. It's pretty resilient. You'll know the dough is ready when you feel like it can't handle any more flour.

- Place the dough in a large bowl, and cover with cling film.* Allow dough to rise for about 45 minutes.

- Punch the dough down to allow some of the air to escape. Cover, and allow the dough to rise for another 45 minutes.

- Remove the dough from the bowl onto a well-floured surface. Cut into 3 equal pieces. Shape and place them in greased and well-floured loaf pans. Cover and allow dough to rise for 1 hour to 1 1/2 hours, until doubled in size.

- Heat your oven to 400°F. Make sure it has come to this heat and stayed there for at least 20 minutes before putting the bread in.

- Bake the bread for about 45–50 minutes. Remove from oven, and allow the bread to cool in loaf pans for about 10 minutes, then remove and place on a grill to cool. Allow the bread to cool completely, about 1 to 1 1/2 hours, before cutting into it.

A hint on dough: Plastic cling film may be wonderful for proofing (rising) dough as it doesn't allow the dough to dry out, but it also means that your dough can occasionally stick to the film. To prevent this, dust the dough with coarser flour when you've placed the freshly kneaded dough into the bowl. Cornmeal, rice flour, or even wheat bran works great and prevents the cling film from sticking to the dough. This is especially useful when you've added the dough to the pans during the final proofing. Otherwise, you could deflate your bread, which, at this stage, is not what you want to do.

du bon pain blanc

1 ½   tasse de lait
2   cuillier à table à sucre,
1   cuil à thé de sel.
2   cuil à table de shortening
2   paquets de levure sèche active compri
½   tasse d'eau de levure sèche
½   tasse d'eau tiède pas chaud

DU BON PAIN BLANC / GOOD WHITE BREAD
MAKES 1 LOAF

"Du bon pain blanc" is the headnote I find in Rosalie's notebook. This bread recipe is one of the few that asks for packages of yeast, something that would have been relatively new for a baker of her era. All of her other recipes called for cakes of yeast, which were much more common at the time. The recipe also calls for milk, buttermilk, and sugar, which would enrich the bread's flavour and extend its shelf life.

This enriched white bread reminds me slightly of an eggless challah, or even French *pain au lait*. It's a great white bread to eat on its own, as toast, and, perhaps best of all, cut into slices and left out to dry overnight for *pain perdu*, also known as French toast.

1 1/2 cups milk
1/2 cup buttermilk
2 tablespoons sugar
2 tablespoons shortening
2 1/2 teaspoons yeast
1/2 cup water, room temperature
1 teaspoon salt
6 cups flour, sifted

- In a saucepan, warm the milk and buttermilk to a gentle simmer.

- Remove the milk from the heat and add the sugar and shortening. Stir to dissolve the sugar.

- Dissolve the yeast in the room-temperature water.

- Add 1 cup of flour into the milk mixture and blend to make a smooth batter.

- Add the salt and yeast water to the batter, and mix thoroughly.

- Add rest of flour, 1 cup at a time, until the dough forms a ball and unsticks from the sides of the bowl.

- With flour-dusted hands, gather the dough into a large ball, and begin to knead the dough on a well-floured surface, adding flour as you go.

- Place the dough in a clean bowl, cover it, and allow it to rest until doubled in size, about 1 1/2 to 2 hours.

- Remove the dough from the bowl. Place on a well-floured surface and knead briefly.

- Roll the dough into a log, and place in a greased and floured loaf pan. Cover, and allow to rise for 1 hour.

- Preheat your oven to 400°F. Place the bread into the oven and bake for 1 hour.

- Remove the bread from the oven and remove from pans. The bread should sound hollow when tapped on the bottom. If not, return to oven for 10 minutes.

- Allow the bread to cool for at least 1 hour before cutting into it.

3 LARD

FOR THE LOVE OF LARD

At a very spry seventy years of age, my father spends each fall out in the woods, hunting with his friends. It's also the one of the few times a year my father gets to eat one of his favourite things—*la graisse de lard,* or salted fatback. It's usually served fried, with the rind, or *couenne,* curling as the fat renders out into the pan. It's delicious—a toothsome mix of salt and fat that crackles at the edges when you bite into it, while the rest melts on your tongue.

My father likes to joke with me that *la graisse de lard* is a mortal sin in our household, usually while winking at my mother. Dad and I both love salted fatback, served with salt fish, boiled potatoes, and boiled turnips. It's a meal I request when I go home and one that my father relishes, since my mother won't make it for him. "It's too much salt and too much fat," she says, lovingly mindful of my father's cholesterol.

I have to admit, I thought about including a recipe on how to salt lard in this book. Fat is delicious. Salt is delicious. Put them together and you have porcine heaven. I realized that the possibility of someone making his or her own salt pork was pretty small. I emailed Jennifer McLagan, the author of *Fat: An Appreciation of a Misunderstood Ingredient, with Recipes* for a little advice on the subject. McLagan's exhaustively researched tome is impressive in its details about every possible form of animal-based fat you could think of, from what type of fat works best for savoury pastry (leaf lard, found around the kidneys) to how to make your own bacon. McLagan does include a recipe for *lardo,* an Italian cured pork fat seasoned with herbs, but no salted pork fatback. I bought a few pounds of fatback, figuring I would try and make salted pork fat at home, and I asked her via email how to make it. Should I brine it? Rub it in salt and wrap it in cloth? Or just salt the shit out of it?

She responded,

> *I am not sure about this, but I think you would just bury it in salt. That is what the Italians do with lardo, plus herbs and spices.*
>
> *The New Orleans chef John Folse told me that when he grew up they had a barrel on the front porch filled with salt and meat and sausages— no refrigeration!! They just dug into the salt and pulled out what*

they wanted. Amazing to think it didn't spoil in the heat they have in Louisiana. They probably weren't as fussy as us.

So as you so eloquently said, "salt the shit out of it," you'll just need more soaking time before you use it.

I don't have a barrel of salt on the front porch, and I realize that very few people will want to know how to cure their own fatback. If you're really interested, I suggest you check out Jennifer's book and website for hints and tips. Thankfully, in Atlantic Canada you can buy fatback in most grocers alongside the other salted pork products.

And yet, I still had five pounds of pork fat I needed to do something with. And the answer was staring me in the face: it was an ingredient in many of the recipes I wanted to make. I needed rendered lard.

Rendered lard was the fat of choice in many Acadian kitchens. It can be used for cooking, baking, frying. Fat was a cheap and nutritious form of energy that kept many Acadians going during the cold winter months.

Today, fat and lard are loaded words. For most of the late twentieth century, animal fats were not appreciated in many grocery store aisles or kitchens, as they were viewed as bad for our health. Today, they are words used coyly by twenty-first-century food lovers, often said with a smirk and an air of superiority, as in "I made this pastry with lard." Thankfully, twenty-first-century science tells us that animal fats aren't as bad as we used to think. (Again, read McLagan's *Fat*. She makes a highly convincing argument as to why butter is better and lard is luscious.)

Today, we don't *need* to render our own lard, let alone use it. Our grocery aisles are full of hydrogenated vegetable shortenings, and our butcher counters offer lard that has been rendered for us. But there is something valuable in knowing how to do so.

The first time I ever rendered my own lard was in fact quite easy, but more importantly it was like travelling back in time. Handling it, cutting it, watching it melt, and waiting for it to render properly made me appreciate the time and effort that went into this process, a very necessary process for many Acadian families until recently. Today the purchasing, use, and eating of foods that use rendered lard are considered to be almost esoteric, even elitist, as they are viewed as unnecessary. But food knowledge is never unnecessary, nor is an appreciation for the work, and lives, that goes into making good, palatable, nutritious food.

And so, I decided to try rendering my own lard. I was talking the talk of discovering my family pantry, so I wanted to know how to walk the walk. Sitting there on my counter, little flecks of pinkish-red flesh dotted the creamy white fat. I cut the fat into cubes, feeling it melt ever so slightly at the warmth of my hands, the knife needing an extra push when it found leftover scraps of skin. Once I finished, it all went into a cast iron pot and then into a barely warm oven.

It wasn't the most glamorous of endeavours. I was worried that the house would smell a little...porky while it rendered. This was not something I could call and ask my mother about. She had never rendered her own lard, and she had no memories of her own mother, Rosalie, doing so. Lard was a word rendered dirty by doctors and the media who talked about the dangers of cholesterol, so it wasn't used as a cooking medium in our house. (Save for pie pastry, but we'll get to that later.) I sent another message to Jennifer who assured me that no, my house would not smell "porky."

She was right. What I did find was a perfect fat that froze very well, that was magnificent for making pie pastry, and that gave a crackling crust to deep-fried foods. I used another batch for making the wild hare *rillettes* I talked about at the start of this book. As for the little pieces of crackling that fell to the bottom of the pot? They became little crunchy bits of pork *confit* that were tossed with a little salt and snacked on while I did the dishes.

RENDERING LARD

You can't talk about Acadian food without talking about pork fat: fresh or salted, it is the traditional fat of choice. Pork fat is also an important culinary and agricultural link to our French origins. Pigs are less resource-dependent than ruminants like sheep and cows who can only eat grasses and specific grains. Their fat is also much more versatile, as it is much more neutral in flavour than other animal-based fats.

Animal fats fell out of favour in the latter part of the twentieth century for various reasons. Doctors and nutritionists warned of links between animal fats and cholesterol, while health issues were purported to arise from eating animal fats, especially pork fat. Pork producers listened and started breeding pigs that had less intramuscular and back fat. Older and heirloom breeds of pigs like Berkshire, Duroc, or Tamworth that were originally bred for their delicious fat became viewed as a quaint throwback or, even worse, undesirable.

The practice of keeping a family pig in the backyard also went by the wayside. Refrigeration and the convenience of larger grocery stores meant that the need—including the necessary work and upkeep—of backyard pigs dwindled, along with the use of pork fat as a cooking and preserving medium. Vegetable-based shortenings were used for occasional bouts of deep-frying, and salted pork fatback was easily available in smaller portions for special occasions. The need for that type of cookery waned. But lard doesn't have to be a dirty word, or the making and rendering of it discouraged. In fact it's quite easy.

How to Render Lard

All you need is fresh pork fat, either from the back or from around the kidneys (also known as leaf lard). You'll also need a good pot. I tend to render lard in a cast iron Dutch oven, but any ovenproof pot will work fine.

To start, chill your fat and make sure your knife is sharp. Cut the fat into pieces, about 1/4-inch in size. The smaller the pieces, the less time it will take for them to render. Preheat your oven to 200°F. Place the fat into your pot and cover with a small amount of water—just enough to cover the bottom of the pot. This will ensure that the fat doesn't scorch, which can lead to bitter or strong flavours. You want the lard to be as neutral in flavour as possible.

Place the pot in the oven, covered, and stir the pork fat every 30 minutes for the first 2 hours, and then every 45 minutes once much of the fat has rendered out. Keep doing so, pressing on the small bits to ensure that everything is well rendered. The amount of time the fat will take to render completely will vary depending on the amount being rendered. You may end up with little crispy bits on the bottom of your pan. Those are essentially crackling, or *gratins*.

Strain the fat into a container, pressing on the cracklings to remove as much fat as possible. They do make tasty little tidbits to be added to dishes or eaten as a snack when tossed with a little salt. The crackling will freeze well for up to three months. Just reheat gently before eating. Trust me on this one.

4 TÊTE DE COCHON

Boudin, made as a sausage. See page
109 for casserole version of recipe.

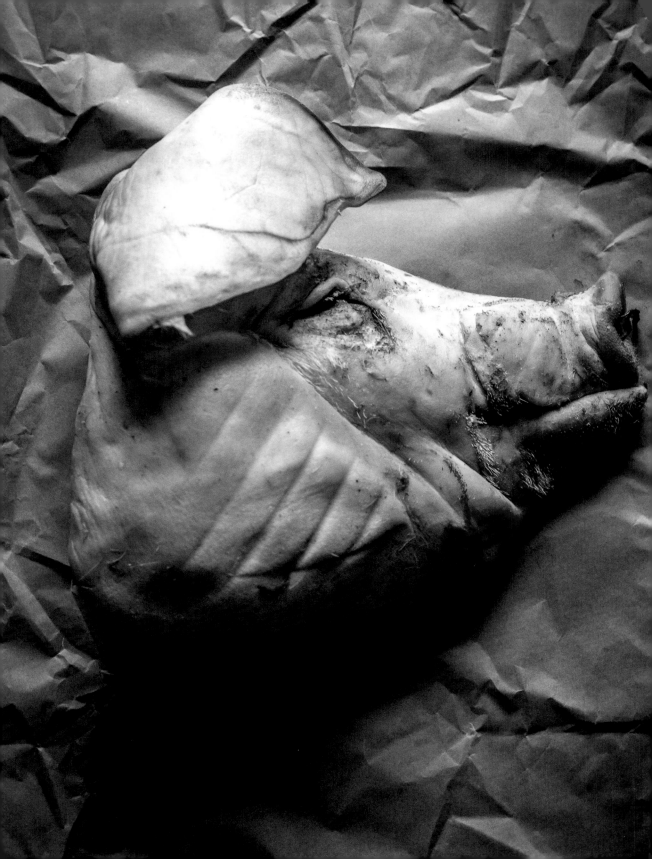

HEAD: THE OTHER MEAT

Like most home cooks in the early part of the twentieth century (and for a long time before that), Acadians were not alone in cooking up every single part of the animal. In November, when Acadians killed their pigs for meat, they used the whole animal. Fresh fats were treasured for deep-frying or rendered out for fresh lard. Much of the meat was salted for eating throughout the winter. I once had a conversation with Edith Thibodeau, who recently turned 102. Edith is a retired schoolteacher and is also the sister of local historian and folklorist Félix Thibodeau (see page 185). Edith told me she remembered her father going to the wharf to buy *"du gros sel,"* coarse salt, from the fish packing plants. The meat would be packed in large wooden barrels, with the coarse salt preserving the meat. The blood would be used to make *boudin,* blood sausage—either in the form of sausages or as a large casserole dish to be eaten at breakfast and lunch. But the head was often turned into *fromage à la tête de cochon,* also known as headcheese or brawn.

I wasn't surprised when I found this recipe amongst all the others. Thankfully, I am somewhat acquainted with cooking a pig's head.

And I think you could be too.

For a year in my early twenties, I stopped eating meat. My reason for going vegetarian was that I had taken issue with the way meat was raised and the ecological impact it usually had upon the surrounding area. I eventually started to eat meat again, and since then the meat I buy comes from small, local, and ecologically and economically sustainable farms. I don't expect everyone to do so, but it's my choice and my reasoning.

The more I read up on and spoke to farmers about farming, animal husbandry, and what happens to animals when they are killed for feeding people, I realized a lot of the animal is often discarded. Most often perfectly edible food is thrown away because it can't be sold or easily turned into an edible product. Pork chops don't grow on dainty little pink hooves, and steaks don't chew cud. I decided to put my money where my mouth was and eat as much as possible of the animal that died for me.

I read up on cooking pig's heads: what to do, what to expect. "You have to shave the ears" said one recipe, which asked to debone an entire head, wrap it in on itself, and then cure it, like you would pancetta. I made *guanciale*, an Italian specialty made of cured pork jowls. I tasted little *croquettes* made from the meat of the head at a restaurant and started to realize how incredibly tasty these little morsels were. Offcuts can be incredibly tasty. They are a lot of work, but then again, if this animal died, the least I could do was make sure none of it went to waste.

I knew I could get a pig's head at my local farmers' market when I saw a vendor selling a dish made from it. A woman named Maureen Legge, who ran a small butcher counter, said that she would indeed sell me a pig's head. I told her I was going to cook it. She looked at me and said, "Are you sure?" before taking my phone number and telling me that it would be ready next week. The next Saturday I showed up at the market bright and early and stood in line with the rest of the customers. Maureen saw me in line and began to dig through cooler after cooler, trying to remember where she had put the head. She knew it would be a fun thing to put on display. By the time I showed up, my order of one large pig's head was waiting on the counter, wrapped in a clear plastic bag.

Its eyes were half open. Its ears were slightly hairy. It had a snaggletooth jutting out of the side of its mouth. Maureen asked me again, "Are you sure?" "Yes ma'am," I said. I took a victory lap around the market with the head underneath my arm. I ran into the very same chef who had cooked up those *croquettes* made from the meat of a pig's head. He looked at me and smiled, congratulating me on my wanting to do this. He warned me that it could be a little intense and that I might want to indulge in a pair of gloves.

By the time I got home, I realized that the head was too big. My usual stock pot was too narrow, and so I had to go and buy an even bigger pot to put the head in. I ended up buying a lobster pot. It's been years since I've bought that pot, and I've yet to cook lobster in it. However, there have been a couple pig's heads and a lot of stock cooked in it.

Pot and pig's head in tow, I headed into the kitchen. I'd gotten used to looking at the head—I was walking the walk, and I was going to eat what I found on that walk. This would be just like all those cooking shows and magazines and books and photos I've seen.

And at first it was. I put the head in the pot, added onions, garlic, carrots, and a bunch of aromatics. I put cold water on top, and onto the stove it went. This was no different than making stock.

Or so I thought.

I could handle looking at the pig's head when it was still uncooked. But by the time it was done cooking, the now very porky broth had done its duty: the skin was a dull greyish brown. It wasn't pretty. And now I had to take the head apart.

I was literally staring my dinner in the face. It gave me pause, but not from nausea or some sense of gastronomic dread. I was reminded of why I had become a vegetarian: 'cause an animal died. This one died so that I could eat. I couldn't turn back now.

I didn't have gloves. I wished I had. At least I knew what I was looking for: meat. And meat there was, more than I thought there would be. The sweetest meat turned out to be near the temple. I narrowly avoided the eyeball, admitting to myself that I was a little grossed out. The tongue was just a giant muscle, ready to be cut into pieces and eaten. I started to understand why people talk about tongue as being tasty. They're right.

Now, as I write this and think about all of the work that would've gone into the raising of an animal—the family pig as it would've been for my ancestors—I know why they would've eaten a dish like this: It wasn't just a question of economy (don't let anything go to waste). It wasn't just one of ethics (this animal died so we should use as much as we can). It was delicious. It was a matter of appreciation for all of those things, as well as all the work that went into its life.

And that's why you can make these recipes. In fact, I know you can.

(Fromage a la tête de Cochon)
l'amotié de la tête de cochon, 5 ou 6
onions cuit avec la viande.
quand il est cuit, metter 2 cuillerée a
clous de giroffe, 2 c. a thé de all spice.
1½ c. a thé de poivre, sel au gout.
½ tasse de Gelatine ou point si o...

FROMAGE À LA TÊTE DE COCHON / HEADCHEESE

MAKES 1 LOAF

This first pig's head recipe is based on the one I found in my family note-books. Interestingly, it suggests powdered gelatin as an option rather than depending on the copious amounts of collagen—which turns into gelatine when cooked—that is already found within the head. Headcheese/brawn/ *tête de fromage* tends to be in the form of pâtés or terrines. It is a large slab of very rich meat encased in one way or another—this time in its own savoury gelatin. Admittedly, beyond the idea of eating a pig's head, a lot of people these days are turned off by the idea of eating savoury dishes with gelatin. Not-so-delicious words like *aspic* are often brought up, and a grey- or brown-looking Jell-O dish with hunks of meat doesn't always invite salivation in diners.

But realistically, this dish is no different than any other pâté you would eat. You just have to get over the idea of eating meat from a head. At the very least, look at it as a challenge: "I will not waste anything." Your grand-mother would be proud.

This recipe, however, gave me very little information on the process of making headcheese, so I went digging into my books and searching online for a little help. First I checked out Fergus Henderson's nose-to-tail cooking bible, *The Whole Beast*, where he describes the dish as a fine lunch. He also suggests reducing the stock, and seasons it with onions, carrots, leeks, celery, garlic, lemon zest, bay leaves, and fresh herbs. I'll leave those options up to you, and you can find out more about Henderson's book in the bibliography.

In the same vein, Henderson suggests using pig's trotters in the dish; they have loads of collagen, which turns into gelatin when cooked. But in my case, trotters are sometimes harder to come by than heads and are often more expensive. I tweeted at Hank Shaw, an avid cook and huntsman and author of *Hunt, Gather, Cook*. He told me that there was plenty of collagen in the pig's head.

And so I've lifted a little from Henderson, a little from my memories, and a little from this old recipe, and come up with what I think is a lovely dish of headcheese. I've left the recipe's seasonings a little on the simple side, but feel free to jazz it up like Henderson does.

A note: Do make sure your pig's head will fit in your stock pot. Seriously. And if your butcher does have pig's trotters, feel free to put a couple in there for good measure. It won't hurt and will in fact increase the amount of gelatine created, yielding a thicker and more flavoursome stock.

1 pig's head
3 medium onions, cut into quarters
2 carrots, chopped roughly
2–3 bay leaves
1 teaspoon black peppercorns
1 teaspoon salted onions (optional)
1–2 chive stalks, chopped finely (optional)
salt to taste

- In a large pot, add all of the ingredients except for the chives. If you have cheesecloth, place the peppercorns, bay leaves, and carrots in there and tie to make a small sachet. This makes it easier to retrieve them at the end. Fill the pot with cold water, until the head is completely submerged.

- Put the pot on the stove and turn the heat to medium-low. You want the water to warm gently, so as not to cloud the liquid too much.

- Bring the liquid up to a gentle simmer, skimming as you go. Keep it at that temperature, and cook for about 2 hours.

- Remove the head and strain the aromatics from the pot. Discard the aromatics. Allow head to cool for about 30 minutes or so, until cool enough to handle.

- Meanwhile, return the broth to the stove, and heat to reduce it by about half. It will smell rather porky.

- Here comes the real work. Remove the meat from the head, namely the cheeks, the bits near the temple (it will be incredibly juicy, in the best way possible), and the tongue. Peel the thin membrane off the tongue. Chop all the meat into uniformly sized pieces.

- Once the broth has reduced, season with salt (or salted onions) and taste. Remember that this dish is usually served cold, so if it doesn't taste salty enough, add a little more.

- Line a dish, such as a shallow casserole or even a bread loaf pan, with cling film. Add the bits of meat and add just enough of the now reduced broth to cover them completely. Add the chives, seal the dish with more cling film, and place in the fridge to gel.

- Serve cold the next day by removing the now set headcheese from its dish.

CROQUETTES MAKES 1 DOZEN OR SO

If you like your pig's head a little more on the crispy side, allow me to introduce you to these wonderful *croquettes*. This is how I prefer to use and serve the meat from a pig's head. It's a litle less work than headcheese, you don't have to worry about your broth, and you get to fry things to a crisp texture. It's not traditional, but it's how I got into eating offcuts, and it's a good entry point for beginners.

Serve with pickled beets or rhubarb preserves, a little bread, and you've got a meal.

1 pig's head
3 medium onions, cut into quarters
2 carrots, chopped roughly
2–3 bay leaves
1 teaspoon black peppercorns

1 cup fine bread crumbs
1–2 chive stalks, chopped finely
salt and pepper to taste

2 eggs
1/2 cup flour
2 tablespoons vegetable oil or lard

- In a large pot, place the head, carrots, onion, and seasonings. If you have cheesecloth, place the peppercorns, bay leaves, and carrots in there and tie to make a small sachet. This makes it easier to retrieve them at the end. Fill the pot with cold water, until the head is completely submerged.

- Put the pot on the stove and turn the heat on to medium-low. You want the water to warm gently, so as not to cloud the liquid too much.

- Bring the liquid up to a gentle simmer, skimming as you go. Keep it at that temperature, and cook for about 2 hours.

- Remove the head and strain the aromatics from the pot. Discard the aromatics. Allow to head to cool for about 30 minutes or so, until cool enough to handle.

- Remove the meat from the head, namely the cheeks, the bits near the temple (it will be incredibly juicy, in the best way possible), and the tongue. Peel the thin membrane off the tongue.

- Chop all of the meat into uniformly sized pieces. Alternatively, if you have a food processor, place it in there and pulse two or three times, no more. You want texture, not mush.

- Take all of the meat and add 1 tablespoon of the fine bread crumbs and the chives. Salt and pepper to taste. Mix together and place in the fridge to chill for 2–3 hours.

- In a shallow bowl, whisk the eggs. In two separate bowls, place the flour and the bread crumbs.

- In a skillet over medium heat, warm up your oil/lard.

- Take the meat out of the fridge and form into patties. Dredge each patty in the flour, then the egg, then the bread crumbs.

- Fry each *croquette* in the oil until crispy on the bottom. Flip over and cook for a couple minutes more.

- Serve immediately.

Boudin, made as a sausage. Those Acadians who
not have access to making sausage at home woul
often bake it in a large casserole dish

BOUDIN MAKES 1 CASSEROLE

The word *boudin* oftentimes evokes images of gumbo, Mardi Gras, and Louisiana. But outside of this area, also known as *l'Acadie Tropicale*, *boudin* is a liberally used term for sausage that is mostly made from offals (organ meats) and that typically includes blood, when it is known as *boudin noir*.

In 2014, I was invited to speak at Le Festival de Clare-té, an arts and culture festival held in Church Point, Nova Scotia. I had been invited to speak on Acadian food traditions, and I wanted to talk about how these traditions are often on the verge of disappearing. I asked the small crowd of people—most of them in their late fifties and sixties—how many of them remember eating *boudin* as a breakfast or lunch staple. Of the two dozen or so people in attendance, about half lifted their hands. I then asked how many of them still ate it. More than half of those hands came down. "And how many of you know how to make it?" All but one or two hands remained in the air. "And that's how your culinary and cultural heritage disappears," I said.

Mention the word *boudin* to Acadians today, and it's often viewed as either an unappetizing dish of the past that we no longer need to eat, or one that is simply too messy to make from scratch. *Boudin* was most often made in the late fall, when pigs were slaughtered and salted for the winter provisions. The blood was collected and made into *boudin*, either as sausages or cooked in large pans, to be cut into pieces and served at breakfast and lunch. It was nutritious and filling and fed many Acadians for generations. With fewer and fewer people having pigs in their back-yards and access to fresh blood, the habit of making and eating *boudin* fell out of fashion. Also, with lack of familiarity came an air of suspicion and disgust around blood and many other forms of offal. We don't "need" to eat these foods anymore, so why should we?

For Delbert Robichaud, making *boudin* is a family affair. Since the early 1940s, Robichaud's Meat Market in Meteghan, Nova Scotia, has been making *boudin* every week. "My mother and uncle made it," he remembers. "We used to make about 150 pounds a week, along with 15–20 pounds of headcheese. We also used to make *cretons* about once a month, and mincemeat in the fall." Today, Robichaud produces only about 150 pounds of *boudin* every two to three weeks. Not only have sales gone down, but the price of the main ingredient—blood—has gone up.

"Younger people don't want to eat it," he says with a bit of sadness in his voice. But Delbert is resilient. "The youth say no, but the elders in the community beg us to make it." Robichaud has a list of regular customers who get phone calls when it's freshly made. "You can't freeze it," he says, "it changes the texture too much." He himself still eats it, saying that *"c'est bon l'enfer."* It's good as hell.

I recognize that not everyone will make this dish or will even have access to fresh blood for making it. But if you can, I strongly suggest that you do. Get a bunch of people together and make some *boudin*, either in the casing (as seen on page 108) or in a large pan. Fry it up in a skillet, serve it for breakfast, or serve it with mashed potatoes with plenty of melted butter.

On making this recipe: If you are able to source fresh pig's blood, you want to make sure it is of good quality and will stay so. In her book *Odd Bits: How to Cook the Rest of the Animal*, Jennifer McLagan gives plenty of great tips on how to store and keep pig's blood. She notes that if you can't use it all, the blood does freeze well for about three months. "Just remember that the liquid expands, so don't fill your containers too full. It…will be darker in colour when thawed." She also recommends shaking it before using it, as it can separate. Just make sure the cover is on tight, unless you want to re-enact a television crime scene.

McLagan also suggests passing the blood through a sieve before using it, to remove any possible clots. "Blood should be used as fresh as possible, preferably the day you buy it or within twenty-four hours. However, it will keep for a couple of days refrigerated if you add a splash of vinegar to stop it from coagulating." Blood works as a thickener and turns dark brown as it cooks, almost chocolate in colour. Be careful when cooking the blood to do so gently, as it can curdle when boiled, creating a sandy and unpleasant texture.

This recipe comes from *Les Dames Patronesses*'s book (submitted by "A patronesse friend," Little Brook) and is intended to be cooked in a large casserole dish. However, if you do have access to a sausage stuffer, feel free to use it.

4 cups blood
4 cups meat (jowls of pork)
10 onions
2 cups milk
1 1/2 cups flour
salt and pepper to taste

(*Author's translation from the French*) The first thing to do once a pig has been killed is to collect the blood, which is very valuable for making *boudin*. Place in a large pan that has a bit of salt placed in it, to help slow down coagulation. Stir well and strain immediately.

Cook meat and onions with small amount of water, stirring frequently. Cook at least 2 hours. Let cool. Mix all ingredients with blood. For best results mix with your hands. Put in a greased pan and bake 1 hour in oven at 350°F.

Proceeding pages: Silverware given to Rosalie Comeau as a wedding gift, still in its original box. It was later maintained by my mother, Jeanne, and now resides in my sister's kitchen.

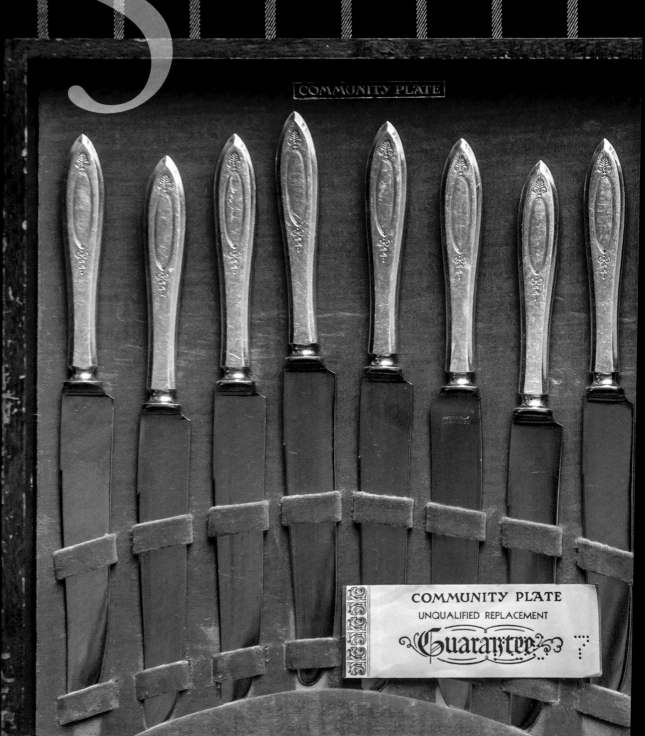

5

SOUPS, SIDES, & STAPLES

COMMUNITY PLATE

COMMUNITY PLATE
UNQUALIFIED REPLACEMENT
Guarantee

Fring Frangs, or potato pancakes recipe on page 152.

BIG MEALS, BIG TABLES

It plays out in the middle of the summer as the table is being set. Last summer's pickles are laid out (hopefully there is more than one kind) and so is the cranberry sauce. The butter just came out of the fridge—condensation is already beading on its sides. There is a carton of molasses just in case someone wants some.

Meanwhile, the oven has been going at 400 degrees for almost three hours. No one seems to care, because there is rápure, *rappie pie, in that oven.*

The word *rápure* refers to that which has been rasped, as in rasped or finely grated potatoes. It is that ingredient which becomes *pâté à la rápure*, commonly known as *rápure*. (For more on this dish see page 141.) It is traditionally made in large rectangular metal pans with raised sides, or *bassins à rápure*. These dishes are anywhere from 12 to 20 inches long, and 6 to 10 inches wide. For the longest time it was also a dish that required a lot of manpower and time to make, the payoff being that the dish was incredibly filling and stuck to your ribs.

Big meals and big dishes often mean big groups of people both making and eating the food. In my house, when rappie pie is made, you know there is some-thing or someone coming: a birthday, a special visitor, a holiday. This time my family decided to make it from scratch. I couldn't have been more than eight. My father and my Uncle François are standing over the sink, shirtless and rasping potatoes over large metal bowls for the rápure. *There is the wet sloshing and scratching sound of the potatoes being rasped over the graters. It is rhythmic, and occasionally syncopated by percussive "ows" as someone grates their fingers instead of the potatoes. There are jokes about there being enough meat from the chicken without bits of fingers in the mix.*

My mother and my Aunt Marie are picking clean the recently boiled chicken meat that is meant to go into the rápure. *I've never seen anyone pick a chicken clean like my mother, doing it while barely looking. She talks and keeps up with everyone, while her fingers dig into the back of the chicken to get the meat out; she makes sure there are no stray bones in the bowl that sits between her knees.*

The rasped potatoes are placed in a large cloth bag that is thicker than cheese-cloth and thinner than a kitchen towel. The pulp is squeezed by hand, rendering and wrenching out the water from the potatoes. It's hard work, as you want to get as much liquid out as possible. The kitchen is not only warm from the bodies, but also from the giant stockpot filled with boiling chicken broth waiting to be used to échaude, or scald, the rasped potatoes. My mother scrapes the potato pulp out of the cloth while my father brings over the steaming pot of stock. They move quickly, as the broth is meant to be as hot as possible when scalding the potatoes, yielding just the right texture. My mother stirs with a wooden spoon to make sure that all of the pulp is well saturated with the hot stock, adding in spoonfuls of salted onions. She takes her electric egg beater and the whisks whir through the now warmed and reconstituted potato pulp. She and my father debate whether or not the texture is right. She defers to him when it comes to the right texture, while he defers to her about seasoning.

Three hours later, we're all sitting at the table. François is laughing about something, my father is slathering butter on his r*âpure, and my mother is saying that she should've added more salted onions. My sister and I tell our mother that it's good, a sentiment echoed by François's wife, Marie.*

The foods brought out during celebrations are often the foods that tell us the most about ourselves, no matter our heritage. A dish at these events isn't just a form of sustenance or a social lubricant, it's an ongoing story brought to the table.

I came across the following description of a picnic, published in *Le Moniteur Acadien* in 1890. It was part of a story about a national Acadian conference that took place in Pointe-de-l'Église, one of the first conferences and conventions organized by Acadians throughout Atlantic Canada. My translation is as follows:

> With the mass having ended, the crowd moves towards the picnic area, where an excellent dinner and entertainment awaits them. There are four tables, each around 200 feet long. The tables threatened to break under the pounds of meats, vegetables and sweets brought by the parishioners, and served by groups of women. Angels armed with patience, and they were most gracious and smiling while they answered to the many requests coming in from all directions. The dinner lasts for two hours, and it is thought that over four thousand people took part of this open air feast.

Although there are no other descriptions of the dishes themselves, the scene painted here is one of conviviality and pride. For these Acadians, eating and being together was a way to reclaim their identity, one that had been marked by their dispersion. This wasn't about being separated by force, it was a force of remembering and recognizing one another.

FRICOT

You don't have to be Acadian to know about, eat, or love *fricot*. This humble soup is known throughout the Maritime provinces. It's found in all kinds of variations of a simple soup based on a meat stock (usually chicken), a hearty portion of said meat, potatoes in one form or another, and a few root veggies (usually carrots). It was so popular that for a while you could even buy it as a canned soup in grocery stores throughout the region. Like any other homestyle soup, every house has their version. In southwestern Nova Scotia they often use salted onions (see page 51) as an aromatic and seasoning, while in New Brunswick it is all about summer savoury (*sariette*). Some versions only have diced potatoes, while some have small *poutines râpées* (not to be confused with the behemoth *poutines* found in New Brunswick, which are a meal unto themselves). Even down in Cajun country, I know of a few people who have made their own Cajun versions. (See page 125 for Cajun *Fricot*.)

A note on stock: The key to a good fricot *is a good stock. It will be your base flavour, so know your palate and what you like so you can make a stock you enjoy. The recipe on the next page is rather simple, staying true to its humble roots. Although this may sound like heresy to some, don't be afraid to add any of your favourite flavourings when making your stock.*

If you love fennel or celery, add it as you would to any other chicken stock. I know many contemporary Acadians who have used shortcuts such as pre-made chicken stock, some poultry seasoning, or even a bouillon cube or two. Having said that, when I make fricot, *this is the one I tend to make.*

If you're making chicken *fricot*, use an old stewing hen for maximum flavour. Wild game is not unheard of for *fricot*, as the preparation lends itself well to tougher cuts of meat, such as wild hare.

FRICOT AUX POUTINES RÂPÉES
CHICKEN *FRICOT* WITH POTATO DUMPLINGS
MAKES ROUGHLY 2–3 LITRES

(Recipe adapted from La Cuisine Acadienne d'Aujourdh'ui *by Les Dames Patronesses de la C.J.A, Inc., July 1963, with thanks to Germaine Comeau.)*

This adaptation was first published in *East Coast Living* magazine as part of a story I wrote on preserving old recipes.

> *This recipe is based on one published in a 1960s booklet by Les Dames Patronesses, a ladies' auxiliary based in the Acadian community of Clare, Nova Scotia. The recipe was spartan, direct, and made for women who knew what to expect in making such a dish. The dumplings are not obvious to make at first glance. This is not to say that they are difficult, but it's not necessarily a type of dumpling that is well known outside of specific regions. There are a few extra details in the recipe method for those who have never made this type of potato dumpling before.*

1 whole chicken, preferably a stewing hen, about 2 pounds
1 onion, minced
3–4 small carrots, diced
7–8 potatoes
2–3 bay leaves
2 teaspoons salted onions (optional)
salt and pepper
oil or butter, roughly 2 tablespoons

- Start by making the chicken stock. Use a stockpot that is large enough to accommodate your chicken comfortably. You want it to be snug in there, but leave enough room for the cooking water. A pot that is too big can lead to a watery and weak stock.

- Cook minced onion in a small amount of oil or butter, adding a pinch of salt to help onion sweat until it turns translucent.

- Add bay leaves, aromatics, and carrots. Stir together until carrots and aromatics become fragrant.

- Sear chicken on all sides in the pot. This will help create a richer stock. Once you've seared chicken, add enough cold water to cover the bird. Bring to a gentle boil, then reduce to simmer, skimming off the scum that will rise to the top to ensure a clear broth. Cook for about 1 hour or until chicken is almost to the point of falling apart.

- Remove chicken from the pot and strain the stock through a sieve, reserving the liquid and discarding herbs and onion.

- Shred chicken, discarding bones and skin.

- At this point you can refrigerate stock and chicken separately overnight and finish the recipe later, or continue on.

- Return the stock to the pot and heat on the stove. While heating, peel and dice 1 or 2 potatoes into small cubes. Add them to your stock. Add the shredded chicken.

- Grate remainder of potatoes as finely as possible, using either the small holes on a box grater or, for an even finer texture, a juicer. If using a juicer, discard the liquid, reserving the potato pulp. If grating by hand, place rasped potatoes in a muslin or cotton bag and squeeze out as much liquid as possible. Place potatoes in a bowl.

- Bring stock to a roiling boil. Add 1/2 cup of boiling hot stock to your grated potatoes and mix quickly. The potato mixture needs to be cooked by the hot stock. Add more stock to potatoes if necessary until it has the consistency of porridge.

- Spoon out portions of potato mixture, about 1 tablespoon at a time, and add them into the boiling soup along with the shredded chicken. Try and make them all the same size for even cooking.

- Cover soup and cook the dumplings for about 10–15 minutes.

- Season soup with salt and pepper. Serve piping hot, with bread and butter.

CAJUN *FRICOT* SERVES 4–6

In 2015, I produced a radio documentary for the Southern Foodways Alliance's (SFA) podcast called *Gravy*. According to their website, the SFA's mission is to document, study, and explore "the diverse food cultures of the changing American South. [Our] work sets a welcome table where all may consider our history and our future in a spirit of respect and reconciliation."

The documentary I produced was called "The Cajun Reconnection," and it told the story of a group of Acadians from Nova Scotia who went to live in Louisiana and came to understand what it means to be Cajun through the food experiences they encountered. But the discussion— and the meals—weren't one-sided. Lucius Fontenot, a native of Mamou, Louisiana, who currently resides in Lafayette, told me how he had spent time in Nova Scotia where he had come across *fricot*, and he felt it could easily handle a bit of Cajun love. Back in Lafayette, Lucius makes *fricot*, but with a twist.

"I add smoked sausage or tasso ham," he said, mentioning that very southern of smoked hams. "I also season it with a good bit of salt, cayenne, and black pepper. That is really it." Although cayenne isn't really a traditional ingredient in Atlantic Canadian pantries, it's hardly an exotic ingredient, and gives a really nice hue to the *fricot*. Cayenne pepper is so ubiquitous in Louisiana that is simply known as red pepper. "Most of us didn't know that there were other hot red peppers made in to red pepper when we were growing up," he joked.

I tend to make this *fricot* with the same potato dumplings in the chicken *fricot* found in the previous recipe, but feel free to make it as you like it.

1 whole chicken, skinned, boned, and cut into pieces
1 onion, minced
1 pound smoked pork sausage*, cut into 1/2-inch pieces
3–4 small carrots, diced

2–3 potatoes, peeled and cut into small cubes
2 teaspoons cayenne
1 bay leaf
2 tablespoons oil or butter
salt and pepper to taste

- Use a stockpot that is large enough to accommodate your chicken comfortably. You want it to be snug in there, but leave enough room for the cooking water. A pot that is too big can lead to a watery and weak stock.

- Over medium-low heat, cook minced onion in a small amount of oil or butter, adding a dash of salt to help the onions sweat until they turn translucent.

- Brown the sausage in the onion. Cook for about 6–7 minutes.

- Add carrots, potatoes, cayenne, and bay leaf. Stir until the aromatics become fragrant.

- In the same pot, sear chicken pieces on all sides. Add enough cold water to cover about 1 inch of the chicken and other ingredients. Bring to a gentle boil then reduce to simmer, skimming off the scum that will rise to the top to ensure a clear broth. Cook for about 1 hour. For an even more developed flavour, remove from the heat and chill overnight in the fridge to allow the flavours to meld.

- Season your soup with salt and pepper. Serve piping hot.

If you're unable to find a good smoked sausage, any good pork sausage made with cayenne (or smoked paprika) is a decent substitute.

MEAT PIES

Along with *fricot* and rappie pie, meat pies are very Acadian. Like many traditional dishes, they vary from region to region and home to home. There is the famous *tourtière* known throughout most of French-speaking Canada and arguably as Acadian as it is Québécois. In Prince Edward Island, meat pies are often hand-held marvels waiting to be savoured. In my home, meat pie is always made with wild hare and a biscuit-like dough. All of these dishes are linked to the holidays, but you shouldn't have to wait all year just to get your fix.

In wanting to pay homage to all of these variations of meat pies, I've decided to go outside of my own home and family and include various types. In addition to my mother's meat pie, you'll find a meat pie from Prince Edward Island, and a *tourtière* from Québec (via the Annapolis Valley).

PÂTÉ À LA VIANDE / MEAT PIE MAKES 1 LARGE PIE, SERVES 8–10

It's not Christmas at my parents' home without this dish. The key ingredient is wild hare, which is darker in colour and more flavourful than domestic rabbit. However, domestic rabbit will do nicely. Unlike the following two "pie" recipes, which are made and eaten as is, this dish is essentially two pieces of biscuit dough with the meat sandwiched between them. Once baked, the "pie" is left to cool overnight, cut into pieces, and cooked in a frying pan with lots of butter. It also freezes very well, and it can be thawed overnight before frying it up for breakfast.

For the filling:

2 hares, cut into pieces
2 tablespoons oil or lard
2 teaspoons flour
1/2 teaspoon salt
pepper to taste

1 onion, minced
1 bay leaf
1 teaspoon salted onions (optional)
2 cups of stock, preferably beef
water as needed

For the pastry:

2 cups flour
3 teaspoons baking powder
1 teaspoon salt
2 tablespoons lard/vegetable shortening
1 cup milk, plus 2 tablespoons for brushing
1/4 cup butter

Tip: I grew up in a household where the meat of the hare was cooked while still on the bone; however, the bones can become quite brittle, so feel free to bone your hare before cooking it.

- Place a large and deep ovenproof skillet on the stove and bring the heat to medium. Add the oil and give the skillet time to warm up.

- Sift the salt into the flour. Add a small amount of black pepper. Dredge the pieces of hare in the seasoned flour.

- Sear the rabbit in the skillet on each side. Remove from the skillet once seared, and add the onion. Cook until translucent. Return the rabbit to the skillet, add the bay leaf and salted onions, if using, and add stock. Add enough water to cover the rabbit if needed, and turn the heat down to medium-low. Cook for 1 hour, or until the meat is tender.

- Remove the rabbit from the skillet and allow to cool. Strain and reserve the broth. Remove meat from the bones and reserve. Make sure you don't have any tiny bones in your meat.

- Meanwhile for the pastry dough, sift flour with the baking powder and salt. Add lard or vegetable shortening and cut into the flour using knives or a pastry cutter until the fat is pea-sized.
- Grease and flour a large (about 9x13-inch) casserole dish. Preheat the oven to 425°F.
- Add milk to the flour, mixing the dough until it just comes together. Cut the dough in half and roll out the first half, large enough to cover the inside of your casserole dish. Place inside the casserole dish. Place the meat on top, and roll out the second half of the dough, just about large enough to completely cover the meat and the bottom layer, and place on top. Brush the top with the remaining 2 tablespoons of milk.
- Place the casserole in the oven and bake for about 30 minutes. It should be slightly browned.
- Allow the rabbit pie to cool overnight in the dish.
- The next day, cut out slices of the pie and break apart into pieces. It's okay if it's messy, as the dish should resemble a hash.
- Heat a large skillet over medium heat and add the butter. Melt the butter until it begins to foam. Add the pieces of pie and stir to break them up.
- Add a small amount of your reserved broth to the skillet. Stir quickly, and then cover to allow the dough to be steamed by the broth. You want it to absorb the flavourful broth.
- Serve immediately with more butter, salt, and pepper.

MARION BUOTE'S MEAT PIE MAKES 9 PIES

In Prince Edward Island, meat pie is a whole different affair. For food writer Melissa Buote, talking about meat pies involves talking about her mother, Marion. Marion married into an Acadian household and took to the making of these pies not long after. Melissa even wrote about this in a story she did for *Saveur* magazine in 2014. This recipe yields at least nine pies, though you can make turnover-style pies, individual serving pies, or cook pies in a cake pan as well. An adapted recipe, more in line with contemporary tastes, was included in the magazine. But for the sake of posterity—and trust that you will be eating all of these pies—here is the original and official recipe for Marion Buote's meat pie.

Note: if by some chance you don't actually eat all of these pies, they do freeze well, up to six months.

For the filling:

4 chickens
3 small beef roasts (approximately 14 pounds)
2 small pork roasts (approximately 7 pounds)
water to cover
12 onions, diced
salt and pepper to taste

For the crust:

15 cups all-purpose flour
6 teaspoons baking powder
3 teaspoons salt
1 pound shortening
6 tablespoons vinegar
3 eggs
3 cups cold water
3 cups of liquid from the pot of meat

- In a large pot place chickens, beef roasts, and pork roasts. Cover with water and boil.

- Cool. Reserve liquid from cooking. Remove skin from chicken and bones from all meat. Chop meat into small pieces.

- Add chopped up meat and diced onions into a large pot, filling the pot with the liquid the beef and chicken were cooked in, reserving 3 cups of liquid to make the crust. Fill until liquid completely covers the meat. Add salt and pepper to taste. Cook until onions are soft.

- For the crust, combine flour, baking powder, and salt. Cut in shortening using two knives or a pastry cutter until the fat resembles small peas.

- In a separate bowl, mix together vinegar, eggs, cold water, and 3 cups reserved liquid from the pot of meat.

- Gradually add the liquid mix to the dry mix, until the dough is moist and just holds together.

- Preheat oven to 350°F. There's no need to do this until the dough is ready, since this is an all-day process. Once you're ready to roll out the crust, get the oven pre-heated.

- Roll out the crust about 1/4-inch thick. Cut dough depending on pie plate, leaving around a 1/2-inch overhang. Fill with meat and a small amount of the liquid. (Don't put too much or your pie will get soggy.) Lay crust over top. Cut vents or prick with a fork. Feel free to make patterns or cut out shapes with cookie cutters. Roll the overhang in on itself to seal the pie. Finish with an egg wash* for a crisp, golden top.

- Once cooked, leave them in the pie pan, but put them on a rack immediately. They can be eaten hot or cold.

* See page 137 for instructions and ingredients for making an egg wash.

TOURTIERE VEAU ET PORC

Pâte: 2 tasses de farine tout usage, 1 c.
à thé de sel, ½ tasse de shortening, 4 c.
à tab. d'eau glacée.

Mesurer la farine, la tamiser avec
sel, y couper le gras jusqu'à ce qu'il soi
de la grosseur d'un pois. Ajouter l'eau
froide et faire la détrempe avec une four-
chette. Rouler dans un papier ciré, mettr

TOURTIÈRE

Tourtière is another of those dishes that is eaten in many French-Canadian households, whether you're an Acadian, Québécois, or Franco-Ontarian. It's just another of those wonderfully filling and festive dishes made with pork as the star of the show; it is also supported by other meats such as beef or veal, which help contribute to a moist pie filling. I wanted to include a few versions of *tourtière*, from a very humble recipe to more elaborate versions.

LES DAMES PATRONESSES TOURTIÈRE MAKES 1 PIE, SERVES 4–6

The first recipe is another of those I found in the *Les Dames Patronesses* collection. It is attributed to Mrs. Robert Belliveau and is a no-nonsense recipe. I've changed a little bit of the wording to make the directions a bit more clear. I'm somewhat surprised that it asks for veal, which isn't always

the easiest meat to gain access to—let alone in 1960s rural Nova Scotia—
but it adds much in terms of lusciousness to the finished pie.

For the filling:

1 pound diced pork shoulder
1/4 pound ground veal (or diced)
3 tablespoons chopped onion
1 teaspoon salt
1/4 teaspoon pepper
1/2 cup warm water
1 tablespoon butter
1/4 teaspoon cinnamon
1/4 teaspoon cloves
pinch of summer savoury
pinch of thyme

- In a skillet over medium heat, melt the butter. Add the pork, veal, and onions and cook about 25 minutes, stirring often.

- Season the mixture with with cloves, thyme, summer savoury, salt, and cinnamon. Taste for seasoning, and adjust if necessary. Allow to cool completely—preferably overnight—in the fridge before preparing the dough.

For the pastry:

2 cups all-purpose flour
1/2 teaspoon salt
1 cup shortening
4 tablespoons ice-cold water

- To make the pastry, measure the flour into a large bowl, then sift in the salt.

- Cut in shortening finely until pea-sized.

- Blend in cold water and mix with fork until the dough comes together.
- Wrap the dough in wax paper and refrigerate for 20 minutes. Divide the dough in two and roll each portion to 1/8-inch thickness.
- Place 1 layer on a 9-inch pie plate, fill with meat mixture, then cover with other layer of dough with cut eyelets.
- Cook 10 minutes at 450°F and then for 25 minutes at 350°F.
- Allow to cool slightly, about 30 minutes, before serving.

AUBE GIROUX'S CLASSIC FRENCH CANADIAN *TOURTIÈRE* MAKES 1 PIE, SERVES 4–6

Aube Giroux grew up in the Annapolis Valley, but her mother was originally from Québec. Aube is the creator of *Kitchen Vignettes*, a series of videos and blog posts for PBS Food, where she creates beautiful videos of food being lovingly prepared. Aube has been nominated twice for a James Beard Award for her videos, in 2014 and 2015. In 2012, she won for Best Single Video at the Saveur Food Blog Awards. These videos aren't dump-and-stir tutorials, nor are they pointless food porn: they are little capsules that tell viewers what each dish means to her. After watching a video she did about *tourtière*, I asked her if she would be all right with sharing her recipe in this book. She was more than kind in saying yes, and I thank her for it. You can read more about Aube and her *Kitchen Vignettes* at pbs.org/food/blogs/kitchen-vignettes/

For the filling:

2 tablespoons olive oil
1 pound ground organic pastured pork
1 pound ground organic pastured beef
1 large onion, finely chopped

2 medium-large baked potatoes, mashed with skins removed
(or about 1 cup of mashed potatoes)
3/4 cup beef or vegetable broth (or just water)
1/2 teaspoon ground cinnamon
1/2 teaspoon ground nutmeg
1/2 teaspoon ground cloves
1/4 teaspoon pepper
1 teaspoon salt

For the butter pie crust:

2 1/2 cups flour of choice (I use a mix of spelt and whole wheat)
1 cup (or 2 sticks) butter
1/2 teaspoon salt
1 cup ice cold water

For the egg wash:

1 egg
1 tablespoon water

- In a large skillet or wok, combine the finely chopped onion with olive oil and sauté for about 10 minutes on medium heat, until onions are soft and golden. With your hands, mix ground pork and beef together in a bowl. Add mixed ground meat to onions and cook for about 10 minutes, stirring it to break up the meat so it doesn't clump together. Add all remaining ingredients (broth, spices, mashed potato, salt, and pepper) and mix together. Reduce the heat to medium-low, cover, and simmer for about 20–30 minutes, stirring occasionally, until most of the liquid is absorbed. Remove from heat. Taste the meat mixture and add a bit more salt, pepper, or spices, to suit your preferences. Cool in the fridge for about 2 hours, until completely chilled.

- To make the pastry, cut the butter into small cubes and chill them so they are very cold. Using a food processor or a pastry blender, chop up the butter into the flour and salt until it is small and crumbly, the size of very small peas. Pour in 1/2 cup of ice-cold water and mix into flour. Add remaining 1/2 cup of water, 1 tablespoon at a time, until the dough comes together into a ball. I find using my hands works best for bringing the dough together and judging whether or not to add more water. The dough should not feel dry and should be pressed into a ball fairly easily, but it should not feel sticky either. Form two balls and flatten them slightly into discs. Wrap and cover them in wax paper or plastic, and let them rest in the fridge for 1 hour.

- Remove from the fridge and allow to sit at room temperature for 5 minutes. Roll out each disc on a floured surface to about 1/8 to 1/4-inch thickness.

- Line a 9-inch pie plate with the first circle of dough. Spoon in all the meat filling, patting it down lightly to compress it a bit. Brush the pie rim with water and place the second circle of dough on top, pressing the edges together to seal. Trim and flute as desired.

- The egg wash is what will give your *tourtière* a golden glow, so don't skip this step! Beat egg and water together and brush the mixture all over the top of the crust and around the edges.

- Cut some steam vents on top of your pie.

- With the rack in the bottom third of the oven, bake at 375°F for about 50 minutes or until the top of the crust is golden.

Mrs. Clarence Dugas getting the evening
meal, Mount Pleasant, Digby, Nova
Scotia, September 1951.
NOVA SCOTIA ARCHIVES

POTATO PROBLEMS

If you're talking about Acadian food, you have to talk about potatoes. Specifically those potato dishes that can sometimes leave people a little confused when it comes to their texture: *râpure*, or rappie pie, and the various *poutines râpées* found throughout Acadian communities in the area.

There is a theory as to how this glutinous form of potato cookery came to be. And it starts in New Brunswick, home of the poutine, or *poutines râpées*. Not to be confused with Quebec's poutine (which is composed of french fries and gravy) or with the small *poutines râpées* often found in *fricot* (see page 122), this poutine is a large dumpling the size of a child's fist, made of grated raw and mashed potatoes. The boiled dumpling strongly resembles a German potato *knödel* (a generic term for dumpling) as well as the Swedish *palt*, which is filled with ham, just like in New Brunswick's salted pork version.

In the 1960s, Father Clément Cormier, an amateur historian from New Brunswick, decided to do some digging into the history of the *poutines râpées*. When talking about the love and devotion Acadians have for the humble dumpling, he said, "you'd think [it was for] a tradition rooted in the past, a heritage from its days of Acadie as a colony, a recipe brought over by ancestors from the old provinces of France."

But Cormier recounts a story he was told, and instead of just being a "someone said something about someone long ago," Cormier actually includes names to place a bit more truth into the mix. The story, told to him by Sister Jeanne De Valois, Mother Superior of the Sisters of Notre Dame du Sacré Coeur, is about Mme Joseph Després, who was the mother of Sister Marie-Lucienne, from the Collège Notre Dame Acadie. (Cormier was later to receive a more detailed version of the story from Sister Marie-Lucienne herself.) Cormier is quoted as saying,

> One day I was told a most surprising story. But after linking it with a historical event, the story seemed credible, and it became the basis of my theory on the origin of our *"poutine rapées."*

> After the First World War, two Germans, freed from a concentration camp, one day at noon hour, rapped at the door of an Acadian home in one of the New England States. To the lady of the house, [...] the

men asked if she would give them food. The housewife agreed, and said she would prepare something special because she suspected that strangers could not like the dish she was preparing for the family.

But the men insisted that she abstain from any trouble and that they would eat whatever was cooking on the stove. When they saw "*poutines rapée*," their faces beamed and they said, "Oh my! This is our national dish."

Cormier goes on to say that he thought the story to be unbelievable but did remember that there were indeed German immigrants who came to Moncton from Pennsylvania in the the mid-1700s. "Putting these two stories together," he writes, "I thought there might be a slight possibility of attributing a German origin to a so-called Acadian specialty. But I was not sufficiently impressed to accept such a theory."

Cormier later came across a book entitled *L'Allemagne Gastronomique*, which included a recipe for *knödels*, a Bavarian dish, which closely resembles *poutines râpées*. Cormier later visited Bavaria, where he told the proprietor of a restaurant that he frequented all about his research into poutines. "They brought my attention to *knödels* on the menu, and they sent the waitress for samples. I was delighted to find my national dish in Germany, so far away from home." Cormier acknowledges that there are some differences in the dish, but states that "the differences are accidental. Essentially they are the same."

RÂPURE / RAPPIE PIE MAKES 1 LARGE PIE, SERVES 4–6

One of the first things you're asked if you ever venture down to the Acadian communities of southwestern Nova Scotia is, "Have you had *râpure?*"

Râpure, or *pâté à la râpure*, is more commonly known as rappie pie in English. It is more akin to a casserole than a pie, but even that is using the term loosely. Its ingredients are modest: potatoes, meat, stock, maybe a little bit of salted onions for flavour, and if you're feeling luxurious, some salteds crunchy and rendered pork fat on the side. But the real deal about rappie pie, that which makes it distinctive and memorable, is the texture.

It is difficult to describe textures, especially those that do not fall under "crunchy" territories. To get people to try and understand what that texture is, it is best to explain how texture is created in a recipe.

Râpure is made by grating or rasping potatoes into a pulp. This was traditionally done by hand on a *râpe* (rasp), which is where the adjective-cum-noun *râpure* comes from. The potato pulp is then placed in muslin bags where the liquid and starch are squeezed out. That very same pulp is then scalded with boiling stock. The mixture is poured into a large metal pan, or *bassin à râpure*, where meat is mixed in. The meat is traditionally poultry, but versions made with bottled clams or wild game such as rabbit, deer, or moose are also known. The dish is then placed in a warm oven for anywhere from two and half to three hours and comes out with a lovely and thin golden-brown crust.

Underneath that crust is a thick gooey potato mass that is somewhere between the look and texture of thick rice porridge and wallpaper paste. That's why those who have never been exposed to it often wonder what is on their plate and why it's there. But trust us. We've been eating this for almost two hundred years, and we're enthusiastic about it. It's our comfort food.

Râpure, or rappie pie, dressed with melted butter and molasses.

The origins of rappie pie are apocryphal at best, interesting extrapolations at worst. Acadians were not known to grow potatoes in any great quantity before the Expulsion, as they were not native to the area, or to Europe. Potatoes are in fact South American in origin, a fact that is forgotten by many people. It has been argued that they probably came to the former colony of Acadie after the deportation of the Acadians, through contact with Irish, English, and notably German immigrants. But history of ingredients aside, how and why did such a dish come to be?

Some people believed that *râpure* was an afterthought, conceived of as way to use up the potatoes that could have been used for their abundant starch. It's hard to deny that rappie pie is a cheap way to feed people, as it is incredibly filling and satisfying. All you need is one chicken, a bunch of potatoes, and you have a large amount of food to feed your family. Although the theory about using potatoes for starch has some merit, it's doubtful that a bunch of people who lived incredibly tough lives as farmers and fishermen would need large amounts of starch for their clothing, even their Sunday best.

The working idea is that *râpure* is in fact Germanic in origin. I've found a couple examples of this, notably what historian and folklorist Félix Thibodeau wrote about *râpure* in his 1978 book *Mélonie et Philomène*, that "the origin of this dish is lost to the ages" (for more about Félix, see page 185). But one small anecdote could shed some light. "Rose Anne Thibodeau, daughter of Moise, from Church Point, [Nova Scotia], went away to the United States where she married a German immigrant. One day she told her husband that she would make a dish from home. When her husband saw the *râpure*, he said, 'My grandmother made something like this.'"

Today, *râpure* is much easier to make. You can purchase pre-grated potatoes in frozen blocks in stores throughout much of Nova Scotia (and even into New Brunswick), showing the migration of the dish—as well as that of the people of southwestern Nova Scotian descent—throughout the area. But to be honest, few people even bother to make rappie pie from scratch these days; even with the potatoes already grated, the work of making a proper stock and knowing how to properly scald the potato pulp is an act that is best learned through repetition. If you don't scald it enough, you may end up with a watery and soupy *râpure*, although some people seem to enjoy it in this manner. (I'm looking at you, residents of Wedgeport, Nova Scotia.) If you don't add enough water, your rappie pie can end up being rather thick and able to be cut into neat squares, which may be easier for some but is not necessarily the most traditional way of cooking and serving the dish. However, it doesn't matter in the end. What matters is making the dish, whether you do so from scratch or use the pre-purchased potato blocks.

It doesn't even matter *where* you make it, as Berndaette Lyle learned a few years ago. Bernadette lives north of Boston, in a suburb called Wakefield, and is one of the people responsible for an annual rappie pie dinner. Lyle grew up in the Acadian village of Quinan, Nova Scotia, but moved to the US in 1963 at the age of thirteen. Even when they were miles away from their Acadian counterparts, they always had rappie pie. "My mom always made sure we had it, as it is a tradition," she says. "We kept that tradition, we knew where we came from and kept in touch with families from there." Years later Lyle joined a Facebook group called Rappie Pie Rules and brought up the idea of having a meet-up for members in the Boston area. "I had fifty people show up to my house," she says. "I had to say no more, I couldn't fit any more. We have friends who came to play music, and nine people brought rappie pie and we had a great afternoon." The meet-up/rappie pie potluck was such a success that when she wanted to do it again, she realized she would have to rent a hall. "It held one hundred people, but we ended up having a waiting list." Lyle planned for the next year, getting an even bigger hall, and more people came, many of them bringing rappie pies to help feed the masses. In March of 2016, the now annual event hosted over three hundred people.

"When you start talking about rappie pie, it's a small world," she says, laughing. "When you start talking to people, the amazing part of the whole thing is having so many Acadians around us." Lyle has met people who are also from her neck of the woods in Quinan, as well as people

A frozen block of rasped potatoes, ready for making into rappie pie. This block is made by D'Eon's Rappie Pie, a third-generation family business based out of Pubnico, Nova Scotia. Their products are sold in major grocery stores throughout the province.

who have family connections to southwestern Nova Scotia. It's through those connections, as well as her own yearly trip to Nova Scotia, that Lyle gets frozen packages of rasped potatoes. Last year she brought back thirty packages.

"With a meal of only three or four ingredients, there are so many different ways to make it," she says. Lyle swears by greasing her pan with salted pork fat and has been known to add a pork chop to her stock pot, as well as dot the top of her rappie pie with small pieces of salted pork, known as *gratins*.

And therein lies the variety of home cooking—everyone has their way. And very often those foodways aren't written down at all, let alone accurately. Writing—let alone finding—a recipe for the making of rappie pie is not exactly an easy task. My own personal and familial materials yielded no such result, as it really was a recipe that was taught in person, rather than written down. It is worth nothing that *La Cuisine Acadienne d'Aujourd'hui* from Les Dames Patronesses does include a recipe, but it asks for "2/3 of pail of big potatoes." This is not exactly accurate or helpful in recreating a recipe. Marielle Cormier-Boudreau and Melvin Gallant's *A Taste of Acadie* offers two recipes, one of which is much closer to *chiard*, a dish of grated potatoes and mashed potatoes that is much more common in Acadian communities in Cape Breton, Prince Edward Island, and parts of New Brunswick.

The bulk of this recipe is loosely based on some notes I received from Peter Boudreau. Peter is a chef with Acadian roots, as his father is from Concession, an Acadian village in Baie Sainte-Marie. Peter didn't grow up in the area, but rappie pie was very much part of his family life. The quantities in Peter's recipe would have been enough to feed an army, but I reduced them slightly to accomodate a family of four, with generous leftovers for reheating. And reheated rappie pie in a skillet with lots of butter is a wonderful thing indeed.

1 (4 pound) whole chicken, preferably a stewing hen
10 pounds potatoes, peeled
2 medium onions, minced
3–4 carrots, diced
2 tablespoons oil or butter
12 cups cold water (or enough to cover chicken in the pot)
2 bay leaves
4 tablespoons minced salt pork (optional)
2 tablespoons salted onions, plus additional 2 teaspoons* (optional)
salt and pepper to taste

- The first thing to do is make the chicken stock. This can be done the day before. In a pot large enough to accommodate your chicken, sauté onions in the butter (or oil) until translucent. Add 1 teaspoon of salted onions if you have them. If not, add a bit of salt to onions to help them sweat.

- Add chicken and cover with cold water, about 12 cups. Add the bay laves and carrots. Cover the pot and bring to boil. Reduce the heat to keep the bird at a gentle simmer. Cook for about 1 hour, or until meat is almost falling off the bone, but not quite.

- Remove the chicken from the pot and strain the stock through a sieve. (At this point you can refrigerate your stock until you need it, or just keep it warm if you plan on making the rappie pie at the same time.)

- Shred the chicken into small pieces, discarding the bones and skin. Set aside.

- Grate your potatoes on a box grater or rasp. Take your time, or you'll end up with bloody knuckles. (Alternatively, you can use a juicer to simultaneously pulverize your potatoes and remove much of the water. The texture will be mildly different, but highly comparable.)

- Place portions of the rasped/grated potato into muslin or kitchen towels. Squeeze out as much of the liquid as you can. You will be adding stock to it afterwards, and you want to get out as much of the liquid as possible. (Tip: Squeeze the potatoes into a large measuring bowl. Let's say you squeeze out 7 1/2 cups of potato water, you should add back in about 10 cups of stock. This is the ratio you're trying to acheive. Adjust accordingly.)

- Bring the stock to a roiling boil. You need it to be as hot as possible to scald the potatoes properly. Heat your oven to 425°F.

- Put the potatoes into a large bowl, big enough to accommodate at least twice its volume. (If you don't have a bowl big enough, do this in batches, making sure to keep your stock as hot as possible for scalding the potatoes.) Break up the potatoes using a hand mixer. Mix in half of the hot stock using a hand mixer, and stir it all together, making sure to moisten the potatoes as much as possible. Mix in the rest of the hot stock and keep stirring. The mixture will thicken, but keep stirring for about 2–3 minutes after adding the last of the stock. Taste for seasoning, adding salt, pepper, and the salted onions as you go.

- Pour enough of the potato pulp to cover the bottom of your casserole dish. Add roughly 1/2 of your chicken, tossing it over the potatoes. Add enough potatoes to just cover the chicken, and then add more chicken, finally covering that with the rest of the potatoes.

- Place the rappie pie into your oven. Bake at 425°F for 30 minutes, and then turn down the heat to 375°F and bake for another 1 1/2 to 2 hours. Occasionally baste the top with butter (or small dice of salt pork) to help the crust brown. The dish is ready when the crust on the top is nice and set and golden brown.

- Serve warm with loads of butter, or possibly a little molasses on the side.

Acadians dig clams at Clementsport, Nova Scotia, for Snow Brothers's packing plant in Digby, July 1951.
NOVA SCOTIA ARCHIVES

CLAM PIE MAKES 1 PIE, SERVES 4–6

When it comes to cookery, it makes sense to use what you have at your disposal. In the case of many Acadians, seafood was common. I was surprised to find next to no seafood recipes in my family notebooks, but it makes sense if you think about it: fish was to be cooked simply, with next to no accoutrements. The beauty of fish is its unadulterated flavour. To add too much to it seems almost like a waste of perfectly good seafood. This is why you'll find lobster often served without drawn butter, while haddock, trout, and mackerel are dressed in nothing but a dusting of flour and quickly sautéed in butter, and the best mussels are steamed in seawater. When it comes to seafood, you shouldn't need a recipe.

There was one exception worth noting, and that was the case of clam pie.

The first time I came across it was in the book from Les Dames Patronesses. I was a bit shocked. Clams in a pie? I called my mother and asked about it. "We never ate it in our house, nor in your father's," she said. Technically the "clams" in this pie are actually quahogs: large bar clams. They have a meatier texture and are much more substantial than their steamer cousins. In our region, clams are often differentiated by size, and so *petites coques* are in fact often steamer clams, while *grosses coques* are in fact quahogs. The very same quahogs are known as *palounes*, a version of the French *palourdes*. Mussels are known as *moucles*, rather than the standardized *moules*.

As for the pie, my mother mentioned that it was a commonly made dish and that Jeanne Cyr, the mother of a childhood friend, was known for her clam pie. Jeanne is well-regarded amongst her friends for her culinary skills and was kind enough to write out her recipe and pass it on to my mother for me to use here. The recipe is straightforward, and it even includes a motherly note: "Call me if you need more explanation." I've recreated the recipe here with a bit more detail and with a very gracious *merci* to Jeanne.

2 pounds quahog meat
1 medium onion, diced
2 cups flour, plus 2–3 tablespoons for thickening
1/2 cup fat* such as lard, butter, or margarine, plus 2 tablespoons
4 teaspoons baking powder
pinch of salt
1 cup milk

- In a skillet large enough to accommodate the 2 pounds of meat, sauté the onions in 2 tablespoons fat over medium heat until translucent.

- Add the quahog meat to the skillet. If using frozen quahog meat, ensure it is thawed before adding it to the skillet. Cook the quahog and onions together for 4–5 minutes, stirring to ensure that any excess moisture from the quahogs is reduced slightly.

- Sprinkle 2 tablespoons of flour to thicken the mixture. If necessary, add another tablespoon of flour, depending on the moisture content.

- Allow the mixture to cool, while you prepare the dough. This will also allow the flour more time to thicken up the sauce from your quahogs.

- In a large bowl, mix remaining 2 cups of flour, the baking powder, and a pinch of salt. Add the remaining 1/2 cup of fat to the flour, using a pastry cutter (or two butter knives) to mix. Alternatively, use a kitchen mixer (on low) to do the same. Add the milk to the mixture and combine. You'll know it's ready to roll out when you can squeeze the dough in your hand and it comes together.

- Preheat the oven to 400°F.

- Flour your rolling surface with a little extra flour. Cut the dough in half. Using a rolling pin, roll out the pastry to about a 1/4-inch thickness.

- Flour an 8x8-inch square pan. Line the pan with one half of the rolled dough, and add the clams. Place the other half of the dough on top, and seal the two halves together by pinching them. Be sure to create small vents in the dough to allow steam to escape, either by poking holes with fork tines or making small slashes with a knife.

- Place the pie in the oven and bake for 30 minutes.

- Remove the pie from the oven and allow to cool for about 45 minutes before cutting into it. Serve warm.

*The original recipe by Madame Cyr asked for margarine as the fat for the pastry. Feel free to use it, but I personally prefer lard or butter. If using lard or margarine, use it at room temperature. Butter should be cold and the dough allowed to rest in the fridge for an hour before rolling. One recipe in the *Dames Patronesses* book even suggested using bacon fat for sautéing the quahogs, something I imagine would yield very tasty results.

FRING FRANGS / POTATO PANCAKES SERVES 2–3

In my house, potato pancakes are known as *fring frangs*. I have no idea why they are named as such, but I do know they were one of the very few dishes that were my father's responsibility. He was the only one who ever made them, and this, in and of itself, made them special to me. My father was the muscle in the kitchen—peeling potatoes for my mother, cutting up squash—with my mother left to the cooking, seasoning, and serving. But with potato pancakes things were different. He grated the potatoes, left the oven at the slightest heat to keep them warm, and had two skillets on the go: one cast iron, the other electric.

There was butter. Lots of butter. Butter hitting sizzling pans, bubbling under potato pancakes the size of my father's workman hands. There were burnt and crisped edges, and a fatherly amount of salt on the potatoes. Bottles of ketchup were in a constant state of burping, their mouths sloppy. It was a little bit of chaos, a little bit of fun, and a lot of Dad.

Potato pancakes are ubiquitous in many households and cultures. From latkes to rösti, it's hard for anyone to resist a crisped and slightly burned edge of potato. When asked for any tips on how to cook them, my father said, "Butter. Lots of butter. More butter than your mother would allow."

Sage advice, Dad.

6 large potatoes
1 tablespoon flour
butter*
3 tablespoons minced onion, or a 1/2 tablespoon salted onions** (optional)
salt and pepper to taste

- Grate potatoes using the largest holes in your grater.
- Remove the excess liquid and starch by placing the grated potatoes into a muslin bag or kitchen towel. Squeeze out as much liquid as possible.

- Place the potatoes into a large bowl, and sprinkle in the flour. (If you're adding onions, this is where you do so.) Mix it in by hand, so that you can feel when all the potatoes have been well covered with the flour.
- Heat a heavy skillet over medium heat. Using your hands, fashion pancakes that are about 1/4 inch thick, and about 2–3 inches wide. Add butter to your skillet, and fry the pancakes in it.
- Once the ends have turned golden brown, flip the pancakes over and cook for another minute or so.
- Serve immediately with pickles, more butter, or whatever suits your fancy. Keep any extras hot in a warm oven.

* In honour of my dad, I didn't include an amount for the butter. Use as little or as much as you would like, just make sure there is always enough to cover the skillet with a thin sheen of fat. Whatever it feels to you is appropriate. And feel free to add a little bacon fat in there while you're cooking.

**The addition of onions would be borderline heresy for my father, as he just wanted to taste the potato and butter. This is a man who eats potatoes raw, like you would eat an apple, so strong is his devotion to potatoes. But I would argue that the addition of onions is a forgivable and tasty sin.

Scalloped Cabbage.

head cabbage   ½ cup bread crumbs
cups white sauce   1 tsp. salt.
tasp. pepper
Soak cabbage in salt water.

SCALLOPED CABBAGE SERVES 3–4 AS A SIDE

This recipe was one of the first I tried to make out of my grandmother Rosalie's notebooks. Beneath the list of ingredients (it was one of the few that contained instructions), was a note saying, "This can be done with any vegetable."* Unfortunately, there was no recipe or directions for the white sauce mentioned in the recipe.

I was gifted Rosalie's *Manuel de cuisine* by my mother a few years ago. The cookbook was one of the few books she brought with her from her time in Trois-Rivières. The *Manuel* is more than just a cookbook; it's a guide on how to stretch a budget, how much nutrition can be garnered from various cuts of meat, and so much more. My mother recalls that her mother often made "*une sauce blanche*" for dishes: a roux-based white sauce. The white sauce found here is very similar to that found in Rosalie's *Manuel,* with a few additions to give it a bit more flavour.

The best kind of cabbage for this recipe is one that will keep its shape when cooked, such as hardy winter white cabbages. Check farmers' markets or your local grocer for cabbages that are good for pickling, as they tend to stand up well to this preparation.

Tip: The great thing about this dish is that you can season your white sauce in all sorts of ways. Traditionally the sauce would be made very plainly, with the nutmeg listed below or summer savoury, but feel free to play around with dried herbs such as thyme, rosemary, toasted caraway seeds, or even a small amount of grated hard cheese. Fresh mushrooms sautéed in the butter (before you add the flour) would be great as well.

1 small cabbage (roughly 1 pound)
1 1/2 cups white sauce
1/2 cup bread crumbs **
2 teaspoon salt
pinch freshly grated nutmeg
pepper to taste

White sauce:

3 tablespoons butter
3 tablespoons flour
1 teaspoon salt
1 1/2 teaspoons summer savoury
1 1/2 cups whole (2%) milk

- Remove the core from the cabbage. Cut the cabbage into strips.

- Add the cabbage to a large bowl, preferably glass or plastic. Drizzle salt on top. Mix thoroughly. Add enough water to cover the cabbage and allow to soak for about 30 minutes.

- Preheat your oven to 375°F.

- Make the white sauce by heating a skillet or sauce pan over medium heat. Add the butter to the pan and sprinkle in the pepper and flour. What you want to do here is cook out the raw flavour of the flour. The butter and flour will combine easily, so make sure you keep stirring it around in the pan to ensure it doesn't burn. Cook and stir for about 2 minutes.

- Add the salt, summer savoury, and milk. Turn down the heat to medium-low. Cook for about 10 minutes, stirring often to ensure that the flour dissolves completely into the sauce.

- Drain the cabbage and place in a baking dish large enough so that the cabbage covers the bottom. Don't worry if it's a little bit snug in there.

- Pour the sauce over the cabbage and mix well to ensure that everything is well coated.

- Cover with bread crumbs. Dust it all with nutmeg.

- Place in oven and bake for 25–30 minutes, or until the cabbage is cooked. It should be soft but still yield slightly to a fork.

- Serve immediately.

* If you are using another vegetable, cooking and salting times will vary. Use your instincts, and your sense of taste.

** The Cornmeal Molasses Bread (page 68) makes excellent bread crumbs.

Turnip 2
Cabbage
$ 1.50 /lb.

NOGGINS CORNER
FARM MARKET
SINCE 1780

Eat Local. Buy Local. Support Lo...

SEAFOOD CHOWDER *À MAME* SERVES 4–6

Almost every time her kids and grandkids make the three-hour trek home to visit, my mother makes seafood chowder. It's a meal that will feed the small army that will soon fill the house. It's a mildly celebratory dish, mostly by virtue of the fact that it means the whole family is together. It's also celebratory for my sister and me, since we don't really have access to seafood as fresh as my parents do.

My parents, Jeanne and Hector Thibault, live in a small village of about three hundred people called Pointe-de-l'Église, or Church Point. You can't escape the ocean when you're there. If you were to stand in the middle of the road in front of their house, you would see Saint Mary's Bay, buttressed by Digby Neck. Their neighbour is a fisherman who often shows up with diver scallops and, occasionally, lobster. Another neighbour up the road will drop by with fresh haddock. Another owns a tiny smoke-house that is no more than a few square feet, just two houses up. You'll occasionally see lightly salted and dried haddock hanging from clothes-lines. The ocean is omnipresent here, in both sight and scope.

My parents know fresh fish. So when *Mame* says she's making chowder, we know that there will be scallops, lobster, and haddock. It won't be overcooked, and the lobster will have been cooked gently in cream before it gets shredded into the pot. There might be a little crab, sometimes fresh, sometimes frozen, a gift that my parents would have received from my cousin Eric. Sometimes the haddock is substituted with another whitefish such as pollock.

We know that there will be white bread and rolls from Le pain de la Baie, a bakery in Saulneriville, just a few villages over. They will have been put into paper bags and warmed in the oven, all to be slathered with giant swaths of margarine. If I'm lucky there is butter, bought for me, as my parents' doctor suggests they try and lower their cholesterol. The family will sit at the rectangular table just outside the kitchen. It was my mother's parents' table, a wedding gift given and received over eighty years ago.

I don't make seafood chowder. I don't have a neighbour who randomly drops off scallops that come in one-pound bags, with sometimes only three or four scallops per bag. My cousin Eric lives too far away for last-minute lobster or crab deliveries. I don't have the habit of cooking lobster, or crab. I leave the seafood chowder–making to the professional. And here is her recipe.

A quick note: I get that not everyone can have access to fresh seafood. Even I don't always have access to all of these things at the same time. So frozen seafood can be substituted where necessary. Just treat it accordingly, making sure to drain any excess water that can come out when the fish is thawing.

1/4 pound butter, divided
1 large onion, minced
2 pounds of potatoes, diced into 1/4-inch cubes
at least one pound haddock, cut or shredded into pieces
at least one pound scallops
at least one pound lobster meat, shredded
1/2 pound crab meat (optional)
1 1/2 teaspoons seafood seasoning/old bay seasoning
1/2 teaspoon paprika
2 bay leaves
1/4 teaspoon salted onions
500 ml blend cream (10%)
2 tablespoons finely chopped chives (optional)

- In a large saucepan, melt 1/4 cup of the butter over medium-low heat. Add the onion, and cook until softened.

- In a large pot, just barely cover the potatoes with cold water. Bring to a simmer and cook until they are about two-thirds done. You should be able to pierce them with a fork, but not all the way through.

- In another skillet, warm up the shredded lobster in the remaining 1/4 cup of butter. Add a touch of paprika for colour, the seasoning, and then the cream.

- Bring the potatoes down to a gentle simmer, and add the haddock. Cook for 1 minute. Then add the lobster and cream.
- Add the scallops, crab meat if available, and the salted onions. Bring the temperature to low, just enough to keep it warm.
- Serve immediately, garnished with fresh chives. And don't forget to have buttered rolls or bread on the table.

re fondre 5 livres de panne; cuire le
re de 5 livres de porc (finement haché)
les longes de flanc coupées en morceaux.
fois la viande bien cuite, y ajouter
oignons hachés, du poivre, du sel, des
es au goût; mélanger à la panne fondue,
t soin de couler la graisse afin que
ui reste de la panne ne soit pas trop
; ajouter un peu d'eau pour cuire les
ons, laisser mijoter sur un feu doux
u'à ce que les boules qui se forment
surface ne fondent pas. Il ne doit
rester d'eau lorsque les cretons sont
à point et ils s'étendent très bien.
u qui a servi à cuire la viande
ilise pour la cuisson des ragoûts.

Mme. P. H. LeBlanc,

Cut into 2-inch cubes 5 lb. leaf-lard and
melt in pot. Cook 5 lb. lean pork and
loins cut into pieces. When meat is well
done, add minced onions, salt, pepper and
other seasoning to taste; blend well and
add to the melted leaf-lard; strain, so as
to remove the fat. Add a little water to
cook the onions, let simmer on low heat,
but not so long as to melt the little fat
balls that come to the surface. There
should not be any water left when the
Cretons are well done. This makes a very
good spread. Use the left-over meat broth
for stew or soup.

Mrs. P. H. LeBlanc,
Little Brook, N. S.

CRETONS   MAKES ROUGHLY 1 1/2 POUNDS

Cretons are distinctively French-Canadian. A type of pâté, they are often
eaten for breakfast on toast. Although they are somewhat omnipresent in
Québec and parts of French-speaking Ontrio and New Brunswick, they are
somewhat less common on kitchen tables in Nova Scotia.

This delicious and easily spreadable pâté is very similar to French *rillettes*
and is a way of preserving meat in its own cooking fat. Unlike *rillettes*,
which is usually made with *confit* (meat that has been preserved in salt
and then cooked in its own fat), *cretons* are usually made from fresh meat.

I found a recipe for *cretons* via Mrs. P. H. LeBlanc from Petit Ruisseau
in *Les Dames Patronesses*. I was surprised to find this recipe in a Nova
Scotian recipe collection, but apparently Mrs. LeBlanc was married to
a doctor from Québec and started preparing the dish for her homesick
husband. I was really impressed by this recipe—published in 1963—
as it asked specifically for leaf lard. This is a very specific ingredient,
and I was surprised to see it listed. Found around an animal's kidneys
(most commonly pork), leaf lard has a different structure than fatback.
It is valued highly for its use in savoury pastries. If you have access to a

butcher or a good meat counter, ask your butcher for leaf lard. If not, regular pork-based fats will do as well.

The recipe here has been adapted and expanded from its original, including notes on how to render the fat. (See page 90 for more details on rendering your own lard.) The reason for the lightness of the spices used in the dish is because you really want to taste the pork, so purchase the best pork you can get your hands on—preferably something that has lived a free-range life. If you're even luckier, find old heritage breeds of pork, such as Berkshire or Tamworth, for this dish.

Mrs. LeBlanc suggests that *cretons* "makes a very good spread," and I have to agree.

1 pound lard, preferably leaf lard
1 pound ground pork shoulder/butt
2 medium onions, diced
1/2 cup of water or broth
salt and pepper to taste
a small pinch of cloves
a pinch of allspice
a pinch of ground cinnamon
1/4 cup fine bread crumbs (optional)

Possible variations: Feel free to sub in some summer savoury for the cloves, allspice, and cinnamon, or to add non-traditional garlic along with the onions.

Note: If you already have rendered lard on hand, proceed straight to the fifth step.

- Pre-heat the oven to 250°F.
- Cut the cold lard into small cubes, about 1-inch pieces. The smaller the pieces, the less time it will take for them to render.

- Place the cubes in an ovenproof dish, preferably a Dutch oven. Add a small amount of water, which will help prevent the fat from scorching. Place the dish in the oven and allow to gently render, stirring every half hour or so to ensure even rendering.

- Strain the fat once it has all rendered. If you have any stray bits floating in the fat, feel free to snack on those, just like you would pork rinds. Allow the fat to cool.

- Preheat a skillet over medium heat. Add the onions and a good pinch of salt and stir. Cook until the onions are translucent.

- Brown the pork in the same skillet as the onions.

- Once the pork has been browned, add the spices and stir well. It should be nice and aromatic.

- Add the liquid to the onions and pork, and bring heat down to a very gentle simmer.

- Cook the *cretons* until the liquid in the dish has evaporated, about an hour. (If using bread crumbs, add them after about 45 minutes of cooking, mixing them in. Cook for another 10–15 minutes.)

- Serve warm or cold, over toasted bread, or on crackers as you would any pâté , with pickles.

6 DESSERTS

Cranberry Pudding. See page 193 for recipe.

MAME, OR HOW I STILL CALL MY MOTHER WITH KITCHEN QUESTIONS

I once asked my mother how to bake a potato.

I had no idea how long it would take. Other than washing it, and possibly sticking it with a fork a few times (so that it wouldn't explode), I had no idea how to proceed.

Mind you, I could make crème brûlée. Because I had a recipe from a magazine.

I (almost) laugh about it now, but I would often call my mother with questions on how to make certain things. I would call her and ask what were the best apples for making pie, how does one cook a trout, what does she use to season her *fricot*, etc.

I never learned to cook from my mother. At least not in the same way that many people learned to cook, with their mothers. I didn't ask her how she made cookies or rolled out perfect pie dough. I didn't ask how she doled out three square meals, seven days a week. When I moved out on my own for the first time, I survived on prepackaged foodstuffs, fried-egg sandwiches, and ridiculous amounts of Jell-O.

But then food became important to me. I began to cook, to explore. I would come home for the holidays, armed to the teeth with recipes from magazines and websites and would make feasts. Once I made a five-course meal for twelve people.

That was the Christmas I tried to make a pie crust using all butter. I had never made a pie crust. My mother is of the lard-based school of pie pastry. Everything is at room temperature, and her hands know when it needs more flour. The amount of pressure needed to bring the fat and flour together is instilled in the nerve endings of her fingers. But playing with flours and fats was very new to me at that time. *Drape the pastry dough over the rolling pin,* said the recipe, armed with a confidence I did not possess. "Uh…*Mame,* what am I supposed to do?" I yelled from the kitchen.

"It's sticking to the counter," she said with a bit of trepidation. "I don't want to ruin your dough." Her face was that of a mother who wants to help, but also doesn't want to ruin her child's project. At this point I just wanted to bake a pie for Christmas dessert, to hell with how it would look. I started to recognize the mild panic my mother would have when she made holiday dinners. The self-critiques of "this is under-seasoned, my pastry is too dry," and everything else mothers who cook for others will say. They want everything to be perfect, to show that their love is as plentiful as the spread they put out before us.

The pie worked. The crust was cobbled together in a few places, but everyone was amazed at the flavour. It didn't look perfect, but the work that went into it made it so.

Mother's Molasses Cake.

... cups sour cream.   *4 cups flour*
" sugar   *2 teasp. soda*
" molasses   *2 cups raisins*
... eggs.   *spices + salt*

GÂTEAU À LA MÉLASSE / MOLASSES CAKE MAKES 1 CAKE

An Acadian pantry is incomplete without molasses. I found many versions of this cake while digging around. It is a very simple yet dignified cake that can easily be eaten out of hand or as a quick snack when you're headed out the door on a cold winter's day. At the end of a meal, it's a great little finish and can be jazzed up with some maple whipped cream or, as one test-baker suggested, a caramel sauce.

The original recipe would have been mixed by hand, but I find that mixing the batter with a hand-mixer or standing mixer yields a better result. I did have to do some playing around with this recipe, as the original version did not state what kind of cake pan was used. The recipe here suggests using a 10x10-inch cake pan, with a baking time of 45 minutes. If you don't have a cake pan big enough to accommodate that space, a couple of loaf pans used for baking bread, or a bundt cake pan may be your best bet. Be sure to adjust your cooking times if you use another cake pan size. The molasses and baking soda reacting together will give the cake its rise, so be sure you have enough room for the cake to do so, with at least a 3/4-inch space. Otherwise you'll find yourself with cake batter splattered all over the bottom of your oven. Be sure to grease your cake pan *very* well, otherwise the cake will stick to it; I tend to grease the pan as well as add parchment paper, to make sure it doesn't.

2 cups molasses
1 cup lard or shortening
4 cups flour
2 teaspoons cinnamon
1 teaspoon all spice
2 teaspoons baking soda
1 teaspoon salt
1 cup milk
1 tablespoon fresh ginger (optional)

- Preheat your oven to 375°F.

- Grease a 10x10-inch cake pan, and then dust generously with flour. Alternatively, add greased and floured parchment paper and place into cake pan.

- Using the paddle attachment on your mixer, fold the flour and lard together on low speed until completely combined, about 4–5 minutes.

- Add the molasses, cinnamon, fresh ginger (if using), and allspice, and mix on low. Make sure to occasionally stop and scrape down the sides of the bowl to ensure all the molasses, lard, and seasonings are blended.

- Add the baking soda and salt, then the milk to the batter, and stir until well incorporated.

- Pour the batter into the pan, and place into the oven.

- Bake for 50 minutes, or until the cake has receded from the edges of the pan and a toothpick placed in the centre comes out clean. Depending on the size of your pan, it may take a bit more or less time. Just keep checking until it comes out nice and clean.

- Leave cake in pan for about 20 minutes, and then invert onto a rack. Serve on its own, or as a dessert with Maple Whipped Cream (page 176), Easy Caramel Sauce (page 177), or Brown Sugar Sauce (page 202).

Maple Whipped Cream MAKES 1 CUP

Many thanks to test-baker extraordinaire Lisa Brow for her idea of a maple whipped cream with this dish, and for the suggestion of baking it in a bundt cake pan.

1/4 cup icing sugar
1 cup whipping cream
2 tablespoons maple syrup

- In a bowl, sift the icing sugar over the whipping cream.

- Start whipping the cream until soft peaks form.

- Add the maple syrup and continue whipping until stiff peaks just start to form. Serve immediately in dollops on Molasses Cake.

Note: A great way to get kids to help with baking is to take all of the ingredients and place them in a Mason jar. Seal the jar carefully, and give it to the kids to shake the dickens out of it, until it becomes whipped cream. They may need a bit of help from an adult, but it's a quick and easy way to get kids involved in the process.

Easy Caramel Sauce MAKES JUST OVER 1 CUP

Caramel sauces come in all sorts of varieties. This is one I've adapted from various recipes, until I got it to where I wanted it. If you like a thicker caramel, add less whipping cream. For thinner, add a little more. Just be sure to not step away from your range as sugar burns quickly, and you may have to start all over again if your caramel burns. Also, be careful when adding the cream to the pan as it will steam and the caramel will bubble and rise.

1/2 cup white sugar
1 cup whipping cream
2 tablespoons cold salted butter (optional)

- Add the white sugar to a dry saucepan. Allow the sugar to melt undisturbed over medium-low heat, until it starts to become a thick syrup.

- At this point, stir occasionally to make sure you don't get any hotspots, leading to bitter or burnt caramel flavours. Wipe away any stray sugar granules with a wet pastry brush.

- Watch the caramel as the colours change. You're looking for a nice deep tan, similar in colour to butterscotch. If you feel like it's getting too dark, pull it off the burner.

- Remove the caramel from the heat, and add the whipping cream. It will bubble and rise, but will quickly calm down.

- Return to medium-low heat, and stir to ensure that the caramel has dissolved into the cream.

- Pass the caramel through a sieve, and add the cold butter if using. Stir until incorporated, and serve warm.

BLANCMANGE / SEAWEED PIE (DONE TWO WAYS)

If you grew up in the Atlantic Provinces, you probably remember a certain television commercial from the early '90s featuring two young kids from Toronto visiting their coastal-living grandparents. The kids are enjoying a supper of fried bologna with their grandparents, when the idea of dessert is brought up. One of the kids offers up the suggestion of cheesecake, but the stern grandfather simply says, "Pie. Seaweed pie." The kids on the screen—and at home, one would guess—scrunch up their noses at the idea. "Well you have to be open to new things," answers the grandmother lovingly.

Or maybe it's about being open to old things.

Seaweed pie is in fact what is known in many Acadian homes as *blancmange*. This dish is a beautiful example of how Acadians shared many pantry staples with other cultures. It's where Acadian and Irish cultures meet: with our tastebuds. The word *blancmange* is French for "white food," a nod to the uniform whiteness of this dessert. But Irish moss (*mousse d'Irlande* in French) is the main ingredient in this dish. Also known as "carrageen" in the British Isles, (which stems from the Irish word *carraigín*, which means little rock), Irish moss is easily found on the sandy expanses of Maritime shores. In fact, this dish is known as Carrageen pudding in Irish homes.

At first glance, Irish moss is unassuming. It can be found near the shore with its tangled and curled masses of white, purplish-black, and grey tendrils. It resembles tiny bunches of lettuces, dusted with a briny sheen. I can remember seeing large swaths of this beautiful sea vegetable laid out on black tarps, sometimes behind people's houses, or even on expanses of back roads. The tarps would be pulled off the road when cars needed to pass. I didn't know anyone who cooked with it but was told of people who harvested and sold it to food companies. As a child, I was told it was used as a stabilizer in making ice cream. It is generally flavourless, which makes it a wonderful gelling aide in all sorts of foodstuffs.

Years later I did a story for *East Coast Living* magazine about edible seaweeds—or sea vegetables as they are now called—and came across Goldie and Gilbert Gillis. This couple from Prince Edward Island does tours of the shore near their home and teaches people how to harvest and use Irish moss in cooking. The recipe below is an adaptation of the recipe that Goldie Gillis contributed to that story. I've also included a simpler version, for historical purposes, found in *Les Dames Patronesses*'s cookbook.

On sourcing the ingredients: Getting my hands on Irish moss wasn't exactly obvious as I don't live within walking distance of a pristine coastline where I can go and pick it myself. I tried using dried Irish moss, which is available in many beer- and wine-brewing stores, but unfortunately the moss was rather musty in odour, as was the resulting blancmange. Thankfully a vendor at the Halifax Seaport Market named Hana Nelson from Afishionado Fishmongers found a local forager to supply her with all sorts of sea vegetables, so she was selling Irish moss along with her own seafood wares. I picked some up and, lo and behold, the wonderfully jiggly dish was soon in my fridge.

A note on the recipes: The first recipe, an adaptation of Goldie Gillis's that first appeared in *East Coast Living* magazine, has the *blancmange* set in a graham cracker crust. The second has it served in individual serving-sized moulds. The third, which I call Acadian Pannacotta, is an adaptation I made in my own home, using higher-fat dairy, such as buttermilk for tang, or 10% coffee cream for a richer dessert.

Also be aware that the vanilla will be the predominant flavour in the dish, so ensure you have good stuff in your pantry.

SEAWEED PIE MAKES 1 PIE

For the crust:

11/4 cup graham crumbs
1/4 cup white sugar
1/3 cup softened butter

For the filling:

2/3 cup fresh Irish moss
4 cups milk
1/4 cup sugar
1 teaspoon vanilla

For the crumb crust
- Mix the ingredients together well in a bowl, making sure to achieve an even texture.
- Press into a greased pie plate and chill for at least 2 hours.

For the *blancmange*
- Soak the moss in cold water for 15 minutes.
- Rinse the moss thoroughly, then drain. Check for stray bits of sand or small stones.
- In a pot, combine the milk, sugar, moss, and vanilla and bring it all to a gentle simmer.
- Allow the mixture to simmer for 20 minutes.
- Strain the liquid to remove any solids. Allow to cool slightly, for about 10 minutes.

To assemble
- Remove the pie crust from the fridge.
- Pour the *blancmange* over crumb crust and cool. Serve with fresh fruit in season.

IRISH MOSS *BLANCMANGE* MAKES 1 PIE
(Reprinted with permission from the Dames Patronesses cookbook, recipe attributed to Mrs. H. B. Comeau, Belliveau's Cove, Nova Scotia.)

1/3 cup fresh Irish moss
4 cups milk
1/4 teaspoon salt
1 1/2 teaspoon vanilla

- Soak moss 15 minutes in cold water to cover—drain, and add to milk. Cook in double boiler for 30 minutes. The milk will seem bit little thicker than when put on, but if cooked longer, *blancmange* would be too stiff. Add salt and flavour. Strain.

- Fill individual moulds first dipped in cold water. Chill. Turn on glass dish, surround with fruit. Serve with sugar and cream.

Baling Irish moss, Wedgeport, Nova Scotia, c. 1954
NOVA SCOTIA ARCHIVES

ACADIAN PANNACOTTA MAKES 6–8 SERVINGS

The first time I made *blancmange*, it instantly reminded me of panna-cotta, the Italian dessert. Pannacotta is a dish known for its distinctive wobble created by the addition of gelatin to warm cream that is then set. *Blancmange* works in the same way, but in this case the gelling agent is the Irish moss. To be honest, I wasn't a fan of pannacotta until I made it with buttermilk, from a recipe I found in New York chef Gabrielle Hamilton's cookbook *Prune*. Her version also includes sweet/sour/bitter lemon compote.

I found myself one day with a leftover litre of 10% blend cream. I tried making the *blancmange* with the higher-fat-content dairy, and voila! A creamier dish. I topped it with some rhubarb conserves I had in the fridge but thought it would be fun to fill the ramekin dishes with a little bit of the conserves as well. The tang with the rhubarb worked incredibly well. And so, Acadian pannacotta was born.

The ingredient list here can be varied according to your tastes and what you have available. Buttermilk will of course have a tangier flavour, while heavier creams will give you a more luxurious version. Feel free to play around, even creating blends of the two. As for the fruit conserves on top, use whatever you have at your disposal. Only be sure that the fruit conserves will set on top. This version adds extra gelatin or Irish moss to ensure the conserves sets.

Note: If you're using a conserves that has lots of fruit chunks in it, and are worried about having to fish out pieces of Irish moss, you can always introduce the Irish moss in a cheesecloth bundle, for easy removal.

1 cup Rhubarb Conserves (see page 197)
1 cup fresh Irish moss
4 cups buttermilk or 10% blend/cream
1/4 cup sugar
1 teaspoon vanilla

- Soak the moss in cold water for 15 minutes. Rinse the moss thoroughly, then drain. Check for stray bits of sand or small stones.

- Warm the conserves in a pot over medim-low heat. Add one-third of the Irish moss and bring to a very gentle simmer. Let it simmer, stirring often, for about 10 minutes.

- Remove from the heat and allow the mixture to cool for about 10 minutes. Strain and allow to cool to room temperature.

- In a fresh pot, add the dairy, sugar, and vanilla. Stir over medium heat, ensuring that the sugar crystals have dissolved. Bring to a gentle boil.

- Add the remaining Irish moss, and reduce heat to a gentle simmer. Allow to simmer for about 20 minutes, stirring occasionally to prevent the dairy from scorching.

- Pass the liquid through a strainer to remove the Irish moss. Allow to cool for about 20 minutes.

- Pour the cooled dairy into the fruit-filled ramekin moulds. Place in the fridge, and chill until set. You'll know they're ready when they have a gentle wobble to them.

- Dollop the rhubarb conserves on top of the pannacotta, and serve.

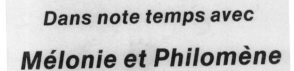

Dans note temps avec

Mélonie et Philomène

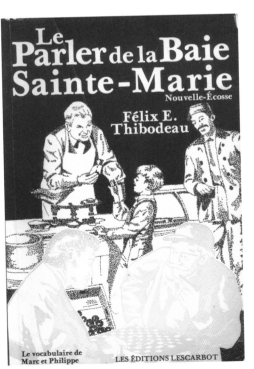

Le Parler de la Baie Sainte-Marie

Nouvelle-Écosse

Félix E. Thibodeau

Le vocabulaire de Marc et Philippe

LES ÉDITIONS LESCARBOT

Félix E. Thibodeau

FOLKLORE, FOLKWAYS, AND FÉLIX

You never know where a recipe will pop up, or what kind of recipe it will be.

The most memorable of all the recipes I discovered wasn't in the notebooks I had received, or in the ladies' auxiliary books I dug through. It was in a book of stories, written by an amateur historian and linguist named Félix Thibodeau.

Félix was known as a folklorist who made it his mission to preserve as much information as he could about the traditions and folkways of the Acadians, particularly those of La Baie Sainte-Marie. For years, he wrote a column for *Le Petit Courrier,* a French-language weekly newspaper that is still in publication. In his column, he wouldn't espouse his own opinions but rather those of two characters (or mouthpieces), named Marc and Phillipe. The column was named *Dans notre temps avec Marc et Philipe* (In Our Day, with Marc and Phillipe), and was a dialogue between the two characters, discussing the past and the old ways of doing things.

Thibodeau published a few books of these dialogues, including all sorts of knowledge on everything from how to collect spruce gum to how to know when a harsh winter is coming. Interspersed in all of these are more than a few stories touching on foodways and cookery. Marc and Philipe even wax poetic about the old varieties of apples that Acadians used to have easy access to, such as the Belliveau apple.

The Belliveau is ready to be picked in early fall, usually around late September. Its origins are less than clear, as some believe that the apple was brought over by the Acadians from France. For a very long time, Acadians used apples for eating and for making cider, but the possibility of one specific strain surviving

(Clockwise from top left) Detail image from one of Félix Thibodeau's books of stories of Marc and Philipe; the author himself; Thibodeau's book that tells stories fom the perspective of Marc and Phillipe's wives, and a dictionary of the particular Acadian French that is spoken in Baie Sainte-Marie. COURTESY OF AUTHOR

the Expulsion of the Acadians is relatively low. Thibodeau, who knew his local history quite well, mentions the idea that the Belliveau came to be in Belliveau's Cove.

In the story "Les poummes" (The Apples), Marc and Phillipe start waxing nostalgic about apples and how it's getting harder and harder to find them. "In our day, there would be one or two trees in each orchard," remembers Marc. During the time Marc and Phillipe are talking about, many families would have orchards of their own, either in their backyard or on a plot of land out in the woods. "We couldn't have lived without an orchard, it was a precious heritage," says Phillipe. "You know that it was old Bear Belliveau who had the first Belliveau in the world." However, author Anne Hutten disproves this in her book, *Valley Gold*. (You can read more about this in the Jeanne's Apple Pie recipe, on page 219).

Thibodeau's work is full of little tidbits that expose the daily life of his ancestors ("If you told Victor to go to the neighbour to get a mother for the vinegar, he wouldn't know what language you're talking"), but he wasn't simply harkening back to the past. Thibodeau wanted to make and keep records of what happened, how things were done, so that others could retrace steps that could easily be lost.

In a book written in the voice of Marc and Philippe's wives, Mélonie and Philomène, Thibodeau includes a chapter that focuses specifically on food traditions and foodways*: "In la Baie Sainte-Marie, there is a difference between a pie and a tart. In general, a tart consists of but a thin pastry at the bottom of the dish, leaving the interior uncovered, while a pie is covered by another layer of pastry."

But the real beauty is in what Thibodeau calls *Poutine au lait vriou*. Thibodeau notes that he was unable to find the origin of the word *vriou*, but he's talking about colostrum. Colostrum (sometimes known as "Bee Stings") is the milk produced by a cow directly after having calved. It is rich in sugars and proteins, and is incredibly nutritious for the newborn calf.

The use of colostrum in cooking is not historically rare, though it is fading. There is a dish in Sweden known as *kalvdans*, which is very similar to the recipe that Thibodeau mentions, and colostrum is often used in making certain cheeses in Italy. Getting your hands on colostrum isn't easy, as cows usually calve during the spring, and the milk is generally reserved for newborn calves to help build up their immune systems. I did once ask for it from a farmer, who told me that he couldn't sell it to me since it wouldn't be pasteurised. "However, if you came to my house, and it was on the table when you came over, I can't say what would happen if I turned my back."

As for the recipe, thanks to Thibodeau, I present it to you, translated in full:

Could this dish be Acadian? For this dessert, take the second pull from the cow who recently calved. Into the milk, add a little flour and cook in the oven for about half an hour. While the dish cooks, you may think you'll have a large quantity of pudding, but once removed from the oven, it flattens into a thin layer. It is eaten as such.

If you ever have the chance to make this dish, please let me know how it turns out.

(Pudding aux Pomme.)

2. tasse farine blanche.

4. c. à. thé de Poudre a Pâte.

3/4. " " " thé de sel. 1. oeuf.

2 c. à. tables de sucre.

2. c. a. tables de beurre ou Saindoux.

assez de lait pour bien melanger.

melanger ingredients secs. ajouter beurre

BAKED APPLE PUDDING MAKES 1 PUDDING

The term "pudding" as it's used in many of these dessert recipes is very much reminiscent of turn-of-the-century English puddings: baked or steamed desserts that were cake-like, and moist desserts that could cook while dinner was being eaten. They were often served with sauces to give them added sweetness, moisture, and flavour. Sauces, such as a hard sauce flavoured with alcohol, were often quickly made. Even plain molasses would do in a pinch.

The beauty of these puddings is that they are incredibly versatile in how they can be flavoured, as well as what kind of additions they can be adorned with. This apple pudding dessert could be easily made with cranberries (fresh or dried) and various other sorts of fruit.

This recipe is another that comes from Eulalie/Rosalie's notebooks. The original recipe was one of the few to offer instructions for how to make the dish. It was probably steamed, which was very much the custom and fashion of the time, but I had never steamed puddings before and realized that it might be intimidating to some home cooks. I decided to bake it instead. The original version asked for white sugar, which I changed to brown sugar for extra flavour, but feel free to use white. I also added two extra eggs for a little more moisture, and I added a little more fat. The original recipe simply asked for "enough milk to blend well," but I have included the more precise measurement of 1 cup. Also, feel free to substitute buttermilk for the milk to add a little more tang.

Note: Because this dish is baked rather than steamed, it is not as moist as its original version. As such, it is suggested that it be served and soaked with the Brown Sugar Sauce on page 202.

2 cups all-purpose flour
1 cup light brown sugar
2 teaspoons baking powder
1/2 tablespoons salt
1/2 cup butter or lard
3 large eggs
1 cup milk
1–2 medium firm-fleshed apples, such as Empire or Jonagold, cut into eighths, or even smaller pieces
2 tablespoons white sugar
1/2 teaspoon cinnamon
1/4 teaspoon allspice
1/4 teaspoon nutmeg

- Preheat oven to 375°F.
- Grease and line a cake dish with parchment paper.
- In a large bowl, sift together the flour, brown sugar, baking powder, and salt.
- Add the lard/butter and mix briefly using a pastry cutter or the paddle attachment on your standing mixer. Mix until the fat is about the size of peas.
- Add the eggs and mix until well incorporated, making sure to wipe down the sides of the bowl. Add the milk, and mix well until the liquid is fully incorporated.
- Add the batter to your pan. You want it to be about 1 inch thick and spread evenly.
- Gently tuck pieces of apple into the batter.
- Blend the cinnamon, allspice, nutmeg, and white sugar. Dust over the batter and place into the oven.
- Bake for 35–40 minutes, until a toothpick comes out clean.
- Serve warm with Brown Sugar Sauce (page 202).

CRANBERRY PUDDING MAKES 1 PUDDING

Cranberries, or *pommes des prés*, grow wild in Atlantic Canada. Although they are available most of the year in grocery stores here in the region, some people, including my parents, still go out and harvest cranberries themselves. The great thing about cranberries is that they freeze incredibly well, and they don't really lose their flavour or texture. They can also be used straight from the freezer. The recipe for this pudding differs slightly than the one for apples, and it asks for more sugar—the natural sweetness found in apples requires less sugar.

2 cups flour
1 cup sugar
2 teaspoons baking powder
1/2 tablespoon salt
1/2 cup butter/lard
3 eggs
1 cup milk or buttermilk
1 1/2 cups cranberries
1/2 teaspoon ground ginger
2 tablespoons brown sugar
1 tablespoon lemon zest (optional; arguably non-traditional, but very tasty nonetheless)

- Preheat your oven to 375°F.

- Grease and line a cake dish with parchment paper.

- In a large bowl, sift together the flour, sugar, baking powder, and salt.

- Add the lard/butter and mix briefly using a pastry cutter or the paddle attachment on your standing mixer. Add ginger and lemon zest and mix until the fat is about the size of peas.

- Add the eggs and mix until well incorporated, making sure to wipe down the sides of the bowl. Add the milk, and mix well until the liquid is fully incorporated.

- Add the batter to your pan. You want it to be about 1 inch thick and spread evenly.

- Gently tuck cranberries into the batter.

- Blend the cinnamon, allspice, nutmeg, and brown sugar. Dust over the batter and place into the oven.

- Bake for 30–35 minutes, until a toothpick comes out clean.

- Serve with whipped cream.

Pudding au Rhubarbe.

Joe-

tasse farine.
tasse de beurre,
Sel
tasse de lait doux.
c. a. thé poudre a pate,
tasse de sucre, canelle.

RHUBARB PUDDING MAKES 1 PUDDING

Amongst the various "pudding" recipes I found in Rosalie's books was
this one. I played with it somewhat to make it a little more refined than its
original form. The first thing was to macerate the rhubarb with orange-
flavoured sugar to give it a bit of a sweet kick and imbue it with a more
complex flavour.

   1 cup fresh rhubarb, cut into 1/2-inch pieces
   1 cup sugar, plus 2 tablespoons for macerating
   1 tablespoon orange zest
   2 cups flour
   2 tablespoon brown sugar
   2 teaspoons baking powder
   1 tablespoon ginger
   1/2 tablespoon salt
   1/2 cup butter or lard
   3 eggs
   1 cup milk or buttermilk
   1/2 teaspoon ground cardamom

- Mix the orange zest into the sugar. It should be nice and fragrant. Add to the rhubarb and allow to macerate for 30 minutes.

- Preheat oven to 375°F.

- Grease and line a cake dish with parchment paper.

- In a large bowl, sift together the flour, sugar, baking powder, ginger, and salt.

- Add the lard/butter and mix briefly using your hands or a pastry cutter. You can also use a paddle attachment on a standing mixer. Mix until the fat is about the size of peas.

- Add the eggs and mix until well incorporated, making sure to wipe down the sides of the bowl. Add the milk, and mix well until the liquid is fully incorporated.

- Strain the macerated rhubarb. Discard the liquid.

- Add the batter to your pan. You want it to be about one inch thick and spread evenly.

- Gently tuck pieces of rhubarb into the batter.

- Blend the cardamom and brown sugar. Dust over the batter and place into the oven.

- Bake for 30–35 minutes, until a toothpick comes out clean.

RHUBARB CONSERVES MAKES 4–6 (500ML) BOTTLES

The initials "BL" were written next to this recipe. I'm not sure who "BL" is, but I would like to thank her very much for this recipe. "Soak overnight 2 quarts rhubarb and sugar," it asks. There were no instructions for how and when to use the citrus, which is used to add pectin to the preserves. I decided to zest and juice the lemon and orange, and then let them macerate along with the rest of the fruit. I'm glad I did, as the smell in the morning was enough of a pick-me-up that I forgot to make coffee. I put the rhubarb straight into a pot to slowly simmer over a couple hours, reducing and thickening it into a tart/sweet jumble that smelled like a cross between poached rhubarb and marmalade. Midway through the cooking, I had a taste, and I may or may not have done a little dance.

A note (or two): The original recipe asks for 1 to 2 quarts of sugar. I only used one, as I found it sweet enough. Once the rhubarb starts cooking down, give it a taste. If you think it can handle a bit more sugar, add a 1/4 cup or so, until it gets to the taste you're looking for. And even though it's not traditional, a vanilla bean that has been split in half and scraped of its seeds never hurt anyone.

When it comes to the citrus fruits, you may want to place them in cheese-cloth before you add them into the pot for cooking. It makes it easier if you wish to remove them from the preserves. I keep mine in as I like the slightly bitter taste I get from them.

2 pounds rhubarb, washed and rinsed
1 lemon
2 oranges
1 pound sugar

- Cut the rhubarb into 1-inch pieces. Place in a large bowl.

- Wash the oranges under warm water, and pat dry. Zest the citrus directly into the bowl with the rhubarb.

- Cut the oranges and lemon in half, and juice them, adding the juice to the rhubarb.

- Add the sugar and the spent citrus halves, and stir well. Place in fridge and allow to macerate overnight.

- The next day place the ingredients from the bowl into a large pot, and turn the heat to medium-low. You will want to bring the rhubarb up to a gentle simmer, making sure to stir often so as not to scorch the sugar or the fruit. Make sure to skim off any scum that rises to the surface.

- Once it's been brought up to a simmer, reduce the heat to medium-low, and stir every 8–10 minutes or so. This helps reduce the amount of liquid, as well as any possible chances of scorching.

- Keep cooking until the rhubarb thickens and reduces slightly, about 90 minutes or so. If you find yourself worrying about it scorching, simply reduce the heat further. It won't hurt, and if anything will allow the liquid to reduce and the flavour to improve.

- Remove the orange and lemon segments if desired and pour the contents into a container. If you want to can/bottle the preserves, follow the instructions on page 33.

- Serve on toast, over ice cream, with yogurt, or whatever your heart desires.

Rhubarbe Pie

at together one egg. 1. cup sugar.
heaping teas flour, pinch of salt,
ir in one cup chopped rhubarbe and
ake between two crusts.

mme F G J Co

RHUBARB CUSTARD PIE MAKES 1 PIE

Rhubarb is a harbinger of spring in Atlantic Canada. It's one of the first hints of the summer sweetness soon to come, even though by itself rhubarb is actually a vegetable and not a fruit. That doesn't matter in Acadian households. After the winter, any excuse for a wee bit of fresh fruit and *douceur* (sweetness) is a welcome thing in many kitchens.

Monsieur F. G. J Comeau, better known as François Grégoire Justinien, was incredibly active in promoting Acadian culture throughout the Maritimes. He started his own newspaper, *L'Écho*, in Meteghan in 1884. He was instrumental forging reconnections with the Cajuns living in Lousiana and people of Acadian descent living in France. He helped in the development of Grand-Pré as a historic site to commemorate the deportation of the Acadians. He served as president of the Société nationale de l'Acadie, or the Acadian National Society. He was also my grandfather Augustin's uncle. Augustin named his first-born son after him.

I have a photo of F. G. J Comeau, standing at Grand-Pré in 1936, along with a large contingent of Cajuns from Louisiana. It was one of the first major events that helped reconnect many Acadians with their Cajun cousins.

Senator Dudley LeBlanc, arriving in Grand-Pré
in 1936, as part of a delegation of Cajuns from
Louisiana who came back to Nova Scotia for the
first time since the expulsion of 1755. This marked
the beginning of the reconnection of many Acadians
with their Cajun cousins. COURTESY OF AUTHOR

And here, in this dusty old blue notebook, I found a recipe for a dish that he probably would have eaten and enjoyed, made by his loving wife. I had never made, let alone had, a rhubarb custard pie. I was a little leery, but this pie became a standard in my kitchen that spring. I could say that I was "testing" the recipe to make sure I got it right, but realistically, I just really fell in love with this pie.

The original recipe asks to "beat together one egg, one cup sugar, one heaping teaspoon flour, pinch of salt. Stir in one cup chopped rhubarb and bake between two crusts." That's all I got.

I wanted to give a bit more instruction than that.

1 pie crust (see recipe on page 215)
2 cups chopped rhubarb, about 1-inch pieces
2 tablespoons milk
1 teaspoon cornstarch
4 egg yolks
1 cup sugar
pinch of salt

- Roll out your pie crust, and place in a round pie plate.
- Preheat oven to 350°F.
- In a bowl, mix the milk and cornstarch together to create a slurry. Add the egg yolks and sugar and pinch of salt and mix until the sugar crystals have dissolved.
- Place the chopped rhubarb on top of the pie crust, making sure to spread it out evenly. Pour the custard over the rhubarb. Gently tap the bottom of the pie on the counter to help eliminate any bubbles.
- Place the pie into the oven, baking for about 50 minutes to an hour, or until the custard is set. You can tell by placing a toothpick into the pie; when the pie is done it will come out clean.

BROWN SUGAR SAUCE MAKES JUST OVER 1 1/4 CUP

Although this reads like something you'd come across in a modern food magazine—use sharp acidic vinegar to enlighten a sweet sauce—it's actually an old way to make an otherwise one-note recipe a little more satisfying and memorable. There are countless variations for this recipe, with some that ask for more sugar or more butter, and some that even add flour instead of cornstarch to help thicken the sauce. For a slightly more bittersweet version, I suggest using demerara sugar, which is essentially sugar that has yet to have the molasses removed from it. Just be careful you don't scorch the sugar when using it, as the colour is already quite dark.

This recipe comes from Eulalie's notebook.

2 tablespoon butter
2 tablespoon cornstarch
1 1/4 cups water
1 cup brown sugar
1/2 teaspoon vanilla
1 teaspoon vinegar

- Over medium-low heat, melt the butter. Add the cornstarch and stir well until smooth and the butter and starch have fully melded.

- In a separate pot, bring water to boil.

- Add the brown sugar to the butter and cornstarch and stir. The sugar will clump at first, but keep stirring so it doesn't burn. You want the brown sugar to be brought to the point where molasses starts to leech out of the sugar and begins to bubble ever so gently.

- Remove from the heat, and carefully stir in the boiling water. Keep stirring until thickened and smooth.

- Strain through a sieve. Add the vanilla and vinegar. Serve hot over desserts like the Baked Apple Pudding (page 189).

Edith's Molasses Cookies

cup molasses

sugar

tsp. ginger

salt

MOLASSES COOKIES MAKES 12–15

To say that molasses cookies are distinctively Acadian is a bit of a stretch, but you can't deny that they would have been made on a regular basis. Molasses is available in easy supply in many Acadian homes, both classic and contemporary. Think about it: the main ingredients were lard and molasses, things which were easy enough to obtain. The cookies can be flavoured and spiced by adding cinnamon, cardamom, allspice, or Chinese five-spice to the batter. You could also dip the balls of dough into sanding sugar before pressing down on them with a fork.

Going through the notebooks, I found five or six different recipes and adapted them to what I wanted. The dough is very forgiving to make, and kids can make it quite easily. Molasses cookies are a type of cookie that works best with lard or shortening rather than butter. So stick with the white stuff, rather than the yellow stuff, when making these.

1 cup sugar
3/4 cup lard
1 cup molasses
1 tsp freshly ground ginger
4 cups flour
2 tsp baking soda
1/4 tsp salt

- Cream the lard and sugar together for about 2 minutes.
- Add the molasses and ginger, and blend well.
- Sift the flour, baking soda, and salt together.
- Add the flour to the mixture until just combined.
- Place the dough in the fridge for about 1 hour.
- Preheat the oven to 375°F.
- Spoon out equal sized portions of the cookie dough, a heaping table-spoon or so, and roll into small balls. Place onto a cookie sheet, and press down gently with a fork.
- Place in oven and bake for about 8 minutes, or until edges are gently crisped.

DATE CAKE

1 cup sugar, ½ cup shortening, 1 cup
sour milk, 1 cup raisins, 1 cup dates,
1 egg, 2 cups flour, 1 tsp. soda, salt
vanilla

Cut raisins and dates finely. Cream
shortening, sugar and egg well. Dissolve baking soda in milk and add alte

DATE CAKE MAKES 1 CAKE
(Recipe courtesy of Les Dames Patronesses, Mrs. Hilaire Dugas, Grosses Coques, NS)

Although they are tropical in origin, dried dates were incredibly common in dry goods stores throughout rural North America. They travelled well and made for more complex flavoured cakes and sweets than sugar or molasses. They also helped baked goods keep their moisture, which extended their shelf life.

This loaf cake is another of those dishes that may not be Acadian in origin but would've been common in many Acadian and Atlantic Canadian homes for much of the early twentieth century.

This date cake recipe was originally published in the *Les Dames Patronesses* cookbook in the early 1960s. The brief instructions and request for sour milk speaks to the probable age of its author, Mrs. Hilaire Dugas of Grosses Coques. I've modernized the recipe's instructions and subbed in buttermilk for sour milk, but otherwise, this is indeed Mrs. Dugas's cake.

1 cup raisins
1 cup dates
1 cup sugar
1/2 cup shortening
1 cup buttermilk
1 teaspoon vanilla
1 egg
2 cups flour, plus 1 tablespoon
1 teaspoon baking soda
1/2 teaspoon salt

- Preheat oven to 375°F. Grease and flour a loaf pan, and/or grease/flour parchment paper to fit interior of said pan.
- Cut raisins and dates finely into small pieces. Dust them with a tablespoon of flour and toss to coat.
- Cream the shortening and sugar for about 3–4 minutes.
- Add the egg, and mix into the shortening and sugar mixture. Make sure to scrape down the sides of the bowl.
- Add the vanilla to the milk.
- Sift the baking soda into the flour.
- Beginning with the flour, alternate adding milk and flour to the mixture. Make sure that all the liquid and/or flour is fully incorporated before adding more.
- Add the dates and raisins, folding them in gently. Be sure to scrape down the sides of the bowl so that all the ingredients are fully incorporated.
- Bake at 375°F until a toothpick comes out clean.

DOUGHNUTS

Unlike my maternal grandmother, Rosalie, whom I didn't know very well, I have very strong—and very food-focused—memories of my paternal grandmother, Josephine (*à P'tit Joseph*) Thibault.

Josephine lived in a yellow house at the bottom of Bonnefant Road, the same road where I grew up. It was the same house where she gave birth to her five children: Odette and Claudette, identical twins, followed by Lorraine, and then Victor and Hector, the other set of identical twins. Hector is my father. Ask him and he will tell you that there was always food on the table and plenty of bread and molasses in the pantry for late-night snacks.

For my sister and me, visits from *Grandmère* were accented by deliveries of doughnuts.

They were always "plain" even if they were anything but. She always delivered them in a plastic bag that once held bagged milk from a nearby dairy. The warm fried dough would steam the inside of the bag ever so slightly, leaving your hands moistened from the condensation as you put them inside. The edges where the dough would hit the hot fat would be crisped, the cakey insides still warm and perfumed with nutmeg.

Although my father would joke that Josephine couldn't make a pie to save her life, we kids thought she was making our lives much better with her doughnut deliveries.

Josephine never wrote down any of her recipes. My mother would often call and ask, "How much of X do I need for making Y?" Josephine would reply, "About as big as a closed fist." Well Josephine's fist was smaller than my mother's, and she couldn't exactly compare over the phone, so for us grandkids the recipe for those doughnuts was lost in the ether.

I found at least seven different recipes for doughnuts in Rosalie's and Eulalie's notebooks, not to mention many more in the old community cookbooks I dug through. What doesn't seem at first to be a distinctly Acadian dish was in fact a big tradition in many Acadian families. Doughnuts require copious amounts of fat for deep frying, and until the advent of vegetable-based fats, pork fat was the frying medium of choice. And when do you have the most fat around? In the fall, when the pigs are freshly slaughtered at *boucheries*. No wonder one of the recipes I found for *boudin* was written directly above a recipe for doughnuts. In fact, I once met an Acadian woman from Prince Edward Island in her early sixties who had fond memories of fresh doughnuts cooked at this time of year. You don't have to wait for fall for doughnuts, and you can fry them in vegetable oil if you like. But if you ever have access to freshly rendered lard (and check out page 90 for directions on how to do it yourself), I strongly suggest it. Go whole hog on those bits of fried dough.

This doughnut recipe (or at least the base of the recipe) doesn't come from Josephine or Rosalie, but from a woman named Agnès, or so says the note in Rosalie's notebook. Agnès was the cousin of Rosalie's husband, Augustin. She was well known in her family for her cooking, but the recipe didn't include any details on what to do, so I asked my friend

Lindsay Cameron Wilson for some help in developing this recipe. I was at a total loss as to how to proceed until she shared her own story about doughnuts and grandmothers. You can find it on her website, lindsaycameronwilson.ca. You should check it out, and try her recipe as well.

AGNÈS'S DOUGHNUTS MAKES 2-DOZEN

1 cup melted and slightly cooled butter
1 cup sugar
3 eggs, separated
4 1/4 cup flour
1/4 teaspoon salt
2 1/2 teaspoons baking powder
1/2 teaspoon baking soda
1/2 cup milk
1 teaspoon nutmeg
1 tablespoon orange or lemon zest (optional)
2 pounds lard or 1 1/2 litres vegetable oil

Equipment:
A doughnut cutter—this will make your life easier.
A hot oil/candy thermometer
A cake rack

- In a large bowl whisk the sugar and egg whites together until the sugar is dissolved. Add the melted butter, citrus zest, if using, and the nutmeg.

- In another bowl, sift together the flour, salt, baking powder, and baking soda.

- Add the flour to the egg and sugar mixture, one cup at a time, adding a small amount of milk to the mixture after each cup of dry ingredients. You want the batter to be firm, rather than soupy. Cover with cling film and allow to rest for 2 hours, or more if possible.

- This is the tricky—but fun—bit. In a cast iron skillet add the lard and melt until it becomes liquid. (Alternatively, simply add the liquid oil.) Make sure you have enough lard to submerge the doughnuts, but still about a 1/2-inch of space from the surface of the oil to the edge of the pan. No one likes a hot oil spill. Bring the heat to medium-high.
- Take about half of the dough, and spread onto a lightly floured counter. Knead the dough gently, and then roll out to about 1/4-inch thickness. Cut out doughnuts using doughnut cutter.
- Make sure your oil is at 375°F. If you don't have a thermometer, take a small amount of the dough and drop gently into the oil. If it sinks, the oil isn't hot enough. If it floats, you're good to go.
- In small batches of about four or five, fry your doughnuts in the oil. When they crisp up on the bottom (you'll see the edges turning slightly brown) flip them over and cook for the same amount of time, generally about 2–3 minutes.
- Drain the doughnuts on a paper towel–covered cake rack.
- Cook the rest of the doughnuts (or perhaps the little bits of dough left, for doughnut holes).

A selection of apples from Ted Hutten, a farmer in the Annapolis Valley. Hutten's mother wrote an entire book about the apples of the Annapolis Valley called *Valley Gold*. It mentions the Belliveau apple, an arguably Acadian variety.

DRIED APPLE CAKE MAKES 1 LARGE CAKE

The need for drying, salting, smoking, and preserving foodstuffs at home waned greatly over the expanse of twentieth-century North America. With that loss went the recipes that told us what to do with those very same foodstuffs. Although these procedures have become trendy amongst professional cooks, we home cooks don't always know what to do with these preserved foods once we have them.

But many cooks have found themselves staring at their pantry, wondering how to feed the hungry mouths that will soon sit at their table. This cake shows what you can make with a few simple ingredients.

The original version, taken from one of Eulalie's notebooks, asked for one cup of sour milk. I've substituted buttermilk for the acidity and also to interact with the baking soda as a leavener for the cake.

2 cups dried apple slices*
2 cups molasses
1/2 teaspoon ground cinnamon
1/2 teaspoon ground allspice
1 cup brown sugar
1/2 cup lard
1 cup buttermilk
2 teaspoons baking soda
4 cups flour

- Soak the apples in water overnight, to allow them to soften.

- Strain the apples, pressing on them to remove any excess water. Chop finely into small pieces.

- In a small saucepan, add the molasses, spices, and apple bits. Bring to a gentle boil, and allow to cook for about 30 minutes. Remove from the heat and allow to cool for 30 minutes.

- Meanwhile, grease a 10x10-inch cake pan, and then dust generously with flour. Alternatively, place greased and floured parchment paper into cake pan.

- Preheat the oven to 400°F.

- Using a mixer, cream at medium speed the brown sugar with the lard. (If using a standing mixer, use the paddle attachment.) Mix for about 4 minutes, until nice and fluffy.

- Turn the speed down, and add the apple and molasses mixture, ensuring to stop occasionally to scrape the sides of the bowl.

- Add the buttermilk and mix until fully blended.

- Sift the flour and baking soda together. Add the flour to the batter, 1/2 cup at a time, making sure each batch is fully incorporated before adding the next.

- Pour the batter into the greased pan and place in preheated oven. Bake for 45 minutes.

*Drying apples is one of the easiest things you can do. Dehydrators are inexpensive and a great investment. All you have to do is peel, slice thinly, and let dry. The real work happens while you wait. Even if you don't have a dehydrator, you can easily do it in your oven by allowing apple slices to dry for 4 to 6 hours at the lowest possible setting.

PIE MAKES 2 CRUSTS, 1 TOP AND 1 BOTTOM

If you are lucky enough to have had a parent (or grandparent) who baked pies, then that pie is probably your benchmark, the one you compare all other pies to.

My benchmark is my mother's pie. I'd eat any pie as long as it was hers. My father is a big fan of my mother's apple pie, and who can blame him? My father maintains a hobby orchard in my parents' backyard with an endless supply of apples, each one yielding various flavours and textures. My sister prefers a wild blueberry pie, and would often ask for it on her birthday in lieu of a cake. I never order pumpkin pie when I go out because they use canned pumpkin, while I grew up in a household where the freezer is always full of pre-cooked and portioned pumpkin purée. I have taken on that practice, so I am ready for pumpkin pie at a moment's notice. "Always be prepared" isn't just a Boy Scout motto—it can easily apply to pie.

I happen to love my mom's pie so much, I did a radio story about it for CBC. I wanted to learn how to make pies the way she does. "I learned from my sister-in-law," she says. "I don't know if I still make it well," she says self-effacingly when I ask her how long it took her to feel comfortable in making pie crust. "Probably a few attempts. After a few years I felt like I had kind of mastered pie crusts."

I learned to bake pies the same way I learned to make anything. By reading books. One book in particular, Rose Levy Berenbaum's *The Pie & Pastry Bible* was instrumental in getting me to understand the hows and whys of pie, but the majority of the pie doughs in her book were all made with very, very cold ingredients: cold butter (if not frozen) and cold water. Berenbaum used next to no liquid. I remember the first time I ever *really* watched my mother make a pie—now armed with somewhat of an under-standing of how things were done—and I marvelled at how she used every-thing at room temperature, and yet her pastry was always nice and flaky.

Pie making doesn't have to be intimidating, but it should be repeated. Try and try again. Besides, you can always eat the mistakes.

This recipe will yield two portions of pie crust—a top and a bottom. It also freezes very well, so feel free to roll it out, place it in a pan, put it in the freezer, and take it out when you need it.

A tip: This pastry works best if you cook it at a higher temperature first (425°F for the first 15 minutes) and then turn it down to 350°F, for approximately 30–40 minutes, until golden brown.

2 cups unbleached all-purpose flour, with more for rolling out the pastry
3/4 teaspoon salt
1 cup lard or vegetable shortening
1 egg
2 tablespoons cold water
1 tablespoon white vinegar

- Sift together the flour and salt in a large bowl.

- Using a pastry cutter (or two butter knives), cut the lard into the flour, until the fat is about the size of peas.

- In another bowl, combine the egg, water, and vinegar. Add to the flour and mix with hands until the dough just about comes together when pressed.

- Flour your countertop with a couple tablespoons of flour. Divide the dough in half.

- Using a rolling pin, roll out the pastry to about 1/4-inch thickness and large enough to fill a 9-inch pie plate.

- Fold the pastry gently in half over the rolling pin, and place in pie plate.

- At this point you can either roll out your remaining pastry to top your pie, or roll it out and place in another pie pan, and freeze.

JEANNE'S APPLE PIE SERVES 6–8

"I don't make it as much as I used to," my mother admits. She says she worries about the cholesterol in the lard, but my father will occasionally mention in his casual manner, "It's been a while since we had an apple pie." And soon enough, one will be made.

My mother uses Macintosh, Gravenstein, or Paula Red for her pies. About mid-fall she likes to use a blend of apples, which gives the pie more variety and substance.

Apple pie is all about two things: the type of apples and the seasonings. The two should play well together and not overpower one another. It's a harmony, not a solo. The type of apple you use can give you varying textures and flavours that can change depending on when the apple is harvested and how long it has been in cold storage.

I'm incredibly lucky to have grown up with an orchard in my backyard. My father started his orchard in the early '80s as something to look forward to in retirement. I know not everyone had apples in their backyard, but if you were to look back at the turn of the twentieth century, many Acadian households did.

Families had particular old varieties that they preferred, with names like Ben Davis, Snow, or Cox Orange Pippin. There is an old variety (which is said to have been preserved by the Acadians) that is known as Belliveau. The history of the Belliveau has gone slightly hazy over the generations. As discussed on page 185, folklorist Félix Thibodeau wrote about them in a story titled "Les Poummes" (The Apples). In it, two characters, Marc and Phillipe, start reminiscing about the apple and how it was getting harder and harder to find. "In our day, there would be one or two trees in each orchard," remembers Marc. "We couldn't have lived without an orchard, it was a precious heritage," says Phillipe. "You know that it was old Bear Belliveau who had the first Belliveau in the world."

In fact, the Belliveau is a transplant from Port Royal, the first major French settlement in North America. In her book *Valley Gold*, author Anne Hutten explains that "[t]he Belliveau was brought from Port Royal to St. Mary's Bay, Digby County, in 1769 or '70 by Mrs. Frederic Belliveau from her father's orchard. Its origin before that time is uncertain." A little bit of Acadian history, still living amongst us in an apple tree.

However, the only customers my father has for Belliveaus are over the age of 80, and this is the same for those who come looking for Ben Davis and other older varieties. "There's no money in those older varieties," explains my father. One of the handful of customers who ask for it, is actually Félix Thibodeau's 102-year-old sister, Edith.

But that lack of sales and interest in older varieties is a sentiment I've heard from most apple growers. It's easier for apple growers to just cut down those trees and graft on newer varieties, like Honeycrisp. Every year someone asks my father for a variety that he no longer grows, as the market wasn't big enough. It's unfortunate and sad to watch an expression of culinary and agricultural heritage disappear with those who once loved it.

The view of heritage apples is changing slowly but surely. There is a great book by journalist and Vermont-based James Beard Award–winning author Rowan Jacobsen called *Apples of Uncommon Character*. It lists 123 different varieties of apples that he finds noteworthy, giving indications on what, how, and where to find them as well as a little history on each apple variety. You'd be surprised how many of these apples are available in Atlantic Canada, and a little saddened by how many of them aren't grown here any longer.

If you're lucky enough to have access to a farmers' market or an apple orchard, do yourself a big favour and buy your apples there. Ask the person behind the counter—or the farmer themselves as they roam around the orchard during a U-pick—what kind of apple you should get. Just tell them what you want to make, and they'll point you in the right direction. Trust them, they know what is good, what is out there.

The recipe for this pie is pretty straightforward and can be made with whatever apples appeal to you. Instead of sweetening the filling with sugar, in our household we tend to use honey. I stick to classics for seasonings: cinnamon and nutmeg. The nutmeg reminds my mother of her own grandmother, who used it in her pies. She still has the old rasp that her own grandmother used when she made this same recipe. Cinnamon was her mother's spice of choice, and so my mother uses both in hers to remind her of the women who cooked before her.

2 pie crusts, rolled out and ready to go (see recipe on page 215)
4–5 medium apples such as Gravenstein, Cortland, Paula Red, Northern Spy, or a mixture
3 tablespoons honey
1 teaspoon cinnamon
1/2 teaspoon freshly ground nutmeg

- Peel, core, and cut the apples into pieces, to whatever size you prefer. Place them in a bowl, dust with the cinnamon and nutmeg, and drizzle with honey. Allow to macerate for 30 minutes.

- Preheat the oven to 425°F.

- Place 1 pie crust into pie pan, leaving a bit of the dough to hang over the side.

- Pour the apples—and any leftover juices—into the pie plate.

- With a pastry brush, wet the edges of the pie dough in the pan. Place the other pie crust over the apples. Trim the edges of the crust, and seal them by either fluting them by hand or pressing them together with the tines of a fork.

- Place the pie into the oven and bake for 15 minutes. Turn the heat down to 350°F and continue to bake for another 30–40 minutes, until the top is golden brown.

- Allow to cool at least for 30 minutes, or until room temperature.

LA TIRE DU COUVENT

4 cups white sugar
4 cups brown sugar
3 cups water
1 tbsp. vinegar
1 tbsp. butter
Cook over a brisk fire and test in cold
water until taffy breaks easily. Put in
buttered pan until cooled. Pull while

LA TIRE DU COUVENT / TAFFY

Sometimes there are recipes that should be left in their original form.
This taffy recipe is one of them. It was one of the recipes that caught my
eye when passing through the *Les Dames Patronesses* book. This recipe
comes courtesy of Mrs. Leo Melanson of Grosses Coques. Although this
collection of recipes was published in 1963, it shows that some people still
cooked in their homes over wood stoves—or at least still had recipes that
were made for just such a thing. I've left the recipe intact, written as it is
found in the book.

> **4 cups white sugar**
> **4 cups brown sugar**
> **3 cups water**
> **1 tablespoon vinegar**
> **1 tablespoon butter**

- Cook over a brisk fire and test in cold water until taffy breaks easily.
- Put in buttered pan until cooled.
- Pull while it is yet soft, and cut into required pieces.
- Avoid placing taffy in damp places.

... le lait et beurre j'arrête ass...

... obtenir une pâte la ...

le mélangeur à vitesse lente

dite au fur et à mesure q...

t la pâte sur la planche a

saupoudrez la farine. pétris...

minute réduiser à ...

beurre fondu et saup...

GLOSSARY

I've always found glossaries in cookbooks to be helpful, not only in coming to understand a place, a people, and its cuisine, but also in seeking those things out. I've benefitted greatly from learning the names of ingredients when out shopping in speciality grocers or having discussions with people about their own regional specialities. I wanted to include a glossary for *Pantry and Palate* to give people insight not only into the Atlantic Canadian foodstuffs found in this book but also into other Acadian food traditions as well.

Different regions not only cook dishes differently, but the vocabulary often used in describing the ingredients and dishes also varies from place to place. That can cause a little confusion. For example, tamarind for me is a jam or preserve made from actual tamarind pulp that was brought to southwestern Nova Scotia from tropical climates. In Acadian communities of Cape Breton such as Chéticamp or Isle Madame, the word *tamarin* is used to describe a form of taffy made from brown sugar. It's entirely possible that at one point such a taffy was made from tamarind, but I haven't been able to find any information about those origins.

I created this glossary to describe some of these differences and highlight certain terms that can be very regional. The two main sources I used come from folklorist Félix Thibodeau's *Le parler de la Baie Sainte-Marie* and author and academic Yves Cormier's *Dictionaire du français acadien*. Thibodeau's is very specific to the region in which I grew up, while Cormier researched throughout Atlantic Canada. Thibodeau's work may be less academic in scope, but it is a more engaging read.

Often the biggest difficulties in creating glossaries—and dictionaries—are questions of phonetics and pronunciation. Acadians throughout the Atlantic region are often distinguished by their accents. We don't sound like the rest of French-speaking Canada, and oftentimes the phonetics, idiomatic expressions, and even verb tenses can be misinterpreted as folksy, or even archaic. But in fact, Acadians are fiercely proud of the way we speak. You could even argue that in the way we speak we are closer to sounding like Molière—the famed seventeenth-century French playwright—than anyone in France. For example, the word green in french is *vert*. But to read Molière in French, one would see the word *vart*. And that is exactly how I, and thousands of people in my region, pronounce that word.

These regional phonetics led to double entries in Thibodeau's book, and variations in spelling in Cormier's. In the interest of fairness to both authors, I have placed their initials after each entry, FT for Thibodeau, YC for Comier. In the case of Thibodeau, some would question whether a phonetic change is worthy of a separate word (*aouène* or *aouaine* instead of *avoine* for oat). I wanted to give readers as much information as possible, and so the more typical French word is placed after the Acadian term.

aouaine or aouène - *Avoine,* oats (FT).

baillarge - *Orge,* barley (FT).

baume - *Menthe.* Mint was most often used in medicinal rather than culinary practices in many traditional Acadian households (FT).

bleuet - In France, one uses the term *myrtilles* for blueberries, but in Acadie and the rest of French-speaking Canada, it's *bleuet*. (YC)

bocouite - A *Francisation* of the English word *buckwheat*, also known as *sarrasin* or *blé noir* (YC).

bordouille - Flour dumplings that are boiled or steamed, served with sugar or syrups. Also known as *grand-pères* (grandfathers).

chancre - Most Acadians refer to various varieties of crab as *chancre* rather than *crabe* (YC).

chenave, genèvre - Ground juniper (YC).

chicaben - Loosely translated, this word, with its roots in the language of the Mi'kmaq, is often translated as "wild potatoes" or "where the wild potatoes grow." The latter definition is also why the village of Pointe-de-l'Église or Church Point used to be known as Chicaben. Potatoes are not indigenous to North

America, and so when the Acadians arrived, potatoes would probably not have been growing wild in the area. It makes more sense to say that these wild potatoes are actually Jerusalem artichokes, also known as sunchokes, or *toupinambours* in French, and locally as *toupines* They are a starchy tuber that grows on the roots of a relative of the sunflower. They have a mild, nutty taste that is reminiscent of sunflower seeds (FT).

clairette - Wild spruce gum that is very clear, hence the name (FT).

dersoué - *Dressoir*, a large hutch, usually built into the wall that contains dishes and occasionally pantry items. The word *dersoué* is also sometimes used in the same way as pantry—an item where both food and dishes are kept. "*Va dans le dersoué pi amène-moi de la confiture au rhubarb.*" / "Go into the pantry and get me some rhubarb preserves" (FT).

doux - Sweets. Although the word *doux* literally means "sweet," it is also used as a noun, rather than an adjective, as it is in English. "*Veux-tu du doux?*" / "Would you like some sweets?" (FT).

eau-de-vie - Alcohol. Although eau-de-vie is known throughout most of the world as a very specific form of distilled alcohol made from a fruit, it is used as a general term for clear liquors and alcohol. "*Veux-tu une drame d'eau-de-vie?*" / "Would you like a drink?" (FT).

échalotes - Green onions, scallions. This is where generations of separation from France causes some confusion. Amongs Acadians of southwestern Nova Scotia, the word *échalote* means green onions or scallions. In France the word *échalotes* is reserved for French shallots, which are a different branch of the allium family. These are the key ingredients in making "*échalotes salées*" or "*oignons salées.*"

fars, fard - Also known as *effard*, the tomalley (or digestive tract) of a lobster (FT, YC).

fayot (fayaux) - *Fèves*, shelling beans. A term mostly used in New Brunswick.

gadelles rouge, gadelles noirs - Red or black currants (FT).

grainnages; aller aux grainnages - Small wild berries; going berry picking (FT).

graton, gratins - Pork cracklings left over from rendering salt pork. Particularly good eaten over rappie pie, or with boiled salt fish and potatoes.

lapin - *Lièvre*, wild hare. The word *lapin* is used interchangeably for both domestic rabbit and wild hare. When someone says they are going "*à la chasse au lapin*" or a dish is made with *lapin*, they are almost always referring to wild hare (FT).

morceau du voisin - An expression meaning "the neighbour's share," traditionally used in conjunction with the butchery (*boucherie*) of a pig. Traditionally most pigs were slaughtered in the fall, and people would help each other with the work. This also led to more people having access to fresh pork rather than salted pork, which was to be a major source of protein during the winter months. The term is also used in any agricultural context when someone lends a hand (FT).

palounne or grosses coques - *Palourdes*, quahogs. These molluscs are often canned or bottled, and used in rappie pie and chowders. The adjunctor muscle, known as the *noucle* (an older version of the word *noeud*, or knot), is especially prized when raw. It is sweet like fresh scallops and is often as large as the scallops that are harvested in the area. A quick note: The road signs in Baie Sainte-Marie are in both English and French. So Pointe-de-l'Église is also known as Church Point. But in the village of Grosses Coques, the name is the same in both English and French (FT).

patate - Potatoes. Next to no one says the more "proper" *pomme de terre* (FT).

petites coques - Soft shell clams, or steamers, are known as such in southwestern Nova Scotia (YC).

toupine - See *chicaben* (FT).

lait verriou or vriou - Also known as colostrum or "bee stings." The first few milkings of an animal, mostly cows, after said animal has calved. This milk is high in antibodies, but it also contains certain sugars and proteins, which lead to its use in making certain dishes throughout the world. In Italy it is used for making cheeses; in Sweden it is used in making a dessert known as *kalvdans*. A similar, pudding-like dish, known as *poutine au lait vriou*, was traditionally made in Acadian homes. With the lack of people having access to such milk—let alone cows in their backyards—the dish is rarely, if ever, made. Félix Thibodeau included a recipe for it in one of his books, *Mélonie et Philomène*. His sister, Edith, who is 102 years old, remembers the dish, and suggested that the second *tire* or pull from the cow is the best for making the dish. This also allows the calf to gain access to the health-giving milk the newborn needs. Edith remembers finding the resulting pudding to be rather rich and not liking it. You can read more about Félix on page 185.

ACKNOWLEDGEMENTS

First and foremost, I'd like to thank my family. My mother, Jeanne, for teaching me the value of cooking for others. My father, Hector, who showed me the connection between nature and sustenance, as well as that importance of hard work. My sister, Ginette, who went on many culinary adventures with me. *Tu me manques.* My brother-in-law, Tim, who walked into my parents' home and sat down and ate *rᐊpure* for the first time with gusto. My nieces, Sophie and Ella, who bring me joy around a table.

Thanks to the rest of the Thibault and Comeau families, with whom I have sat and enjoyed many a meal. Special thanks to 'Noncle François for showcasing the life of a gourmand, and apologies to Tante Lorraine for the pig's head.

Naomi Duguid, who went from being someone I admired from afar to someone I could call on to ask for advice, steer me when I needed it, and believed in me from the get-go. I can't thank you enough.

To Noah Fecks, who made me cry when I saw the images we made together. I'm still pinching myself. Love you, bud.

My friends and former housemates, Ryan Frizzell and Sarah Curry, who housed me for much of the beginning of the writing of this book. It wouldn't be here without your help.

Whitney Moran at Nimbus, who gave me the time and direction I needed. Thanks for being a great editor who knew when to push, and to being open to my ideas.

Patrick Murphy from Nimbus, who sent me an email that would change my life, during a time when I needed a change.

To the editors, publishers, and producers who have supported my work throughout the years: Trevor Adams, Tina Antolini from *Gravy* and the Southern Foodways Alliance, Corie Brown, Alex Kristofcak, Kim Hart MacNeill, Kathryn Hayward, Janice Hudson, Kathy Large, Karon Liu, Allison Saunders, Kyle Shaw, Lukas Volger, Stewart Young, and so many more.

Christina Harnett, who taught me who to think for, rather than who to think about.

Diane Paquette, Sandy Smith, and the gang at CBC Radio in Halifax, who gave me the opportunity to tell stories in a way I couldn't imagine.

Susan Newhook, who kept me focusing.

Jennifer McLagan for making me unafraid of fat.

Tucker Shaw at America's Test Kitchen, for his help and inspiration.

Andrea Weigl, who sent me kind words when I needed them.

Sofia Perez, who believed in me, and told me to stop thinking of myself as a country mouse.

Stephen Sherman Wade, who said the same thing to me, along with a whole lot of other wonderful things no one had before.

Lesley Chesterman, who told me how and when to use the word "great."

Judith Olney, who believed in my idea and told me stories about dinners with MFK Fisher, James Beard, Julia Child, and Richard Olney.

Natalie Robichaud, *qui me fais buster.*

Karen Pinchin, who knows the pain of making headcheese.

Melissa Buote, who reminded me to think from all possible angles, and for her mother's meat pie recipe.

Lindsay Cameron Wilson, for helping me figure out doughnuts.

Lucius Fontenot, for his Cajun *fricot* recipe.

Peter Boudreau, for helping me measure out the proportions for making *râpure*.

Jeanne Cyr, *pour ta belle recette.*

Delbert Robicheaud, for talking to me about *boudin.*

Lisa Brow, for her great baking ideas.

Germaine Comeau, for her help with *Les Dames Patronesses.*

To the food writers and storytellers who inspired me (either personally or through their work) and told me that I was on the right track: Dan Barber, John Birdsall, Fuchsia Dunlop, Barry Estabrook, Kat Kinsman, The Kitchen Sisters Davia Nelson and Nikki Silva, Daniel Klein and Mirra Fine from Perennial Plate, David Leite, Andrea Nguyen, Marie Nightingale, Dan Pashman, Carolyn

Phillips, Nik Sharma, Arlene Stein, Anita Stewart, Michael Twitty, and Grace Young.

And thanks to all of these people who helped, even if they didn't know it: Peter Aikman, Stephen Boudreau, Breton Cousins, the gang at Chives Canadian Bistro, Paul Courtright, Chris deWaal, Rachelle Dugas, *la famille* Durand, Jonny English, Allen Holden, Damian French, Hank Green, Michael Howell, Jeffrey Liberatore, Georgette LeBlanc, Josette LeBlanc, Erik Lilllimagi, Lezlie Lowe and Kevin Lewis, James MacCormack, Megan McCarthy, Robynne Maii, Mark Mendoza, Jon Morse, Kelly Neil, Nadine Ouellette, Chris Patterson, Mike Reynolds, Lia Rinaldo, and Trent Roode.

And last but not least, *le monde de Clare.*

adding the addition of
1 cup raisins, make
glaze frosting.

1 egg
1 cup sugar
3 tablespoon butter
1 cup milk   salt
2 cups flour
4 teaspoonful baking powder

                crown bread
3 cups butter milk
1 cup molasses
cups oat meal

ANNOTATED BIBLIOGRAPHY

Although much of this book came to be due to primary (and somewhat familial) sources, there are multiple books that helped in its making. Some were direct sources, while others were inspirations. I've decided to list both, as
I think it's important to give as much credit as possible, and some of that credit is indirect.

Out of Old Nova Scotia Kitchens, **Marie Nightingale**
For the longest time in Nova Scotia, recipes and cookery practices were told person to person, family to family, or occasionally in community cookbooks. Although these are important, they can often become ephemeral and lost in the ether. Nightingale delved further than just telling people how to dump and stir ingredients together. She gave context and content, giving readers more than just a tasty recipe: she offered them history, character, and the opportunity to transmit generations of foodways outside of their original reach. In 2014 I had the opportunity to conduct the last ever interview with Marie Nightingale, in a story for the website Zester Daily. She said that she loved the piece I wrote about her, and was moved that I understood the impact of her work. She passed away a few weeks later.

A Taste of Acadie, **Melvin Gallant and Marielle-Cormier Boudreau**
Originally published in French in 1975, this tome has been the quintessential Bible for many Acadian cooks and culinary historians, myself included. Thankfully, the book was translated into English in 1991, permitting many an English-speaking Acadian (and their friends) access to these recipes and the information found therein.

Les Dames Patronesses, **Church Point, Nova Scotia**
A resource, a time capsule, this collection of recipes shows readers how homemakers were cooking and baking and living during the 1960s.

Cuisine de Cheticamp, **Ginette Aucoin** and *Travel On*, **Jean Doris LeBlanc**
Two out-of-print books detailing life in the Acadian communities in Cape Breton, I am indebted to these two women for showcasing some of the differences and similarities of Acadian kitchens from one part of the province to the other.

Fat and *Odd Bits: How to Cook the Rest of the Animal*, Jennifer McLagan

McLagan's books are not only exhaustive in their research, but these two in particular tell us how to use animal fats and parts in cuisines from all over the world, and from as many animals as possible. McLagan convinced me to eat more animal fats in more ways than I ever thought possible, let alone healthful. McLagan is a multiple James Beard Foundation Award winner for her cookbooks, including her latest book, *Bitter*.

Anita Stewart's Canada, Anita Stewart

In many ways, Stewart is a living library of Canadian foodways and history—ask her about any topic or traditon from St. John's to Chilliwack, or up in Iqaluit, Stewart has the answers, or at the very least, will know where to send you. *Anita Stewart's Canada* is a treasure trove of information that only hints at the diversity of food traditions—both past and present—that can be found in Canada.

Apples of Uncommon Character, Rowan Jacobsen

Jacobsen's *Apples* is great example of how a simple apple can be more than just a piece of fruit. Jacobsen's devotion to detail—even in his tasting notes—makes this book a must for any serious fruit lover, let alone fans of food history. His other books, *A Geography of Oysters* and *American Terroir*, are must reads for serious food lovers.

The Whole Beast, Fergus Henderson

Nose-to-tail was made into a trend a few years ago in the restaurant world, and Henderson's book is an in-depth look at eating everything you can eat from an animal. Details on history, practicality, and the economics of such cookery are provided in a book that could convince anyone to try eating offals, odd bits, or whatever you want to call them.

Hunter, Angler, Gardner, Cook, also *honest-food.net*, Hank Shaw

Shaw is a renaissance man who knows how to cook what he hunts, gathers, fishes, and gathers. His books, website and Twitter feed are full of helpful hints for any food fan who lives for wild foods.

Pickles and Preserves, **Andrea Weigl**
Weigl's work reflects and reveres the home cook, that often forgotten person in today's celebrity-chef driven media. Weigl was kind enough to not only allow me to share her tips, but she often shares her knowledge and tips online at her website andreaweigl.com.

The Pie and Pastry Bible, **Rose Levy Berenbaum**
Berenbaum's books are an exercise in precision and detail, almost to the point of intimidation. Almost. Berenbaum is the teacher who will tell you about the variables you may encounter, but only so that you, the amateur baker, will be armed and ready before you even turn on the oven. She will make you a better baker.

Valley Gold, **Anne Hutten**
Hutten is a journalist, a mother, and a farmer. She is also a non-stop worker, or so I am told by her son Ted. I am indebted to Ted for telling me about his mother's book, and to Anne herself for the information found within *Valley Gold*.

Dans notre temps avec Marc et Philip; Dans notre temps avec Mélonie et Philomène; Le parler de la Baie Sainte-Marie, **Félix Thibodeau**
Sometimes the most interesting information about food isn't found in a cookbook. It can be found with two old friend telling tales, or even in a dictionary. Any of Thibodeau's works are worth reading for any Acadian, or lover of folkways and traditions.

Whispers of the Past, **Edward S. D'Entremont**
Another example of how local storytelling can tell you more about how people lived and ate than cookbooks. D'entremont waxes poetic about tamarind in his book.

Waste Not, Want Not: A Book Of Cookery, **E. F. "Ted" Eaton**
Eaton's book is one of folklore, foodways, and fun. Not every recipe is meant to be cooked (roasted cow udder, anyone?) but Eaton's research demonstrates the sheer variety of cultural heritages that make up Atlantic Canada.

Loyalist Foods In Today's Recipes, **Eleanor Robert Smith**
The impact that the Loyalists had on the larders of Atlantic Canadian is vast.
Thanks to Smith for collating this information in a tidy package.

Kitchen Vignettes (**kitchenvignettes.blogspot.ca**), **Aube Giroux**
Aube is a filmmaker, an activist, a storyteller, and a cook. Her work has been
featured in such publications as *Saveur*, *The Huffington Post*, *Harper's Bazaar*,
and many more. Aube is currently finishing her first feature, a documentary
called *Modified* about genetically modified foods.

Inspiration

The Mile End Cookbook, **Noah and Rae Bernamoff**
Even though I grew up 300 km from the closest knish, *The Mile End* made me
understand that when it comes to writing a book about a food culture, some
things are universal—like home, and the flavours that are found within.

Hot, Sour, Salty, Sweet, **Jeffrey Alford & Naomi Duguid**
Alford and Duguid's books are the reason I write about food, and the reason
I learned to cook in the way that I do. Researched, yet personal, speaking of
cultures outside their own, yet without a trace of "the exotic" tone often found in
food writing about "ethnic" cuisines, their books are a treasure trove of information for any serious cook, and a resource for those who would be nervous about
cooking the food of another culture. I recommend any and all of their books,
especially Duguid's recently solo efforts, *Burma: Rivers of Flavour* and *A Taste
Of Persia*.

Momofuku Milk Bar, **Cristina Tosi**
It's easy to dismiss a cookbook author for being popular, or for being hyped. But
if that author is actually teaching people to go into their kitchens and learn how
to do things for themselves, they are worth applauding. Tosi's first cookbook
taught me how and why I should measure, yet also gave me options on what to
do when I couldn't. That is something not every book will do.

Heritage, Sean Brock
Brock has made it his mission to preserve as much information as he can about southern cookery, especially that of the Low Country. *Heritage* is not only a book about a cook and his path, but it also paints the broader picture of how so many people, so many ingredients have a greater strength than just one guy in a kitchen. And he's more than happy to let those people shine.

Tartine Bread, Chad Robertson
Robertson's books and breads have become the high benchmarks for bread bakers both amateur and professional. Robertson has spent years doing all the dirty work, arguing how bread really is the staff of life, hearty and sturdy, rather than soft and insubstantial.

Lima, cuire très lentement pendant environ une heure ou jusqu'à ce que la viande et les légumes soient cuits. Verser dans des petits plats de verre allant au feu et recouvrir d'une couche de pâte.

PATE

2 tasses de farine;
1 c. à thé de poudre à pâte;
½ c. à thé de sel;
2-3 tasse de lard ou de graisse végétale;
6 à 8 c. à table d'eau glacée.

Mode de préparation

Tamiser la farine, la poudre à pâte et le sel ensemble. Mêler à la graisse en coupant avec deux couteaux jusqu'à ce que les morceaux soient de la grosseur d'une fève de Lima. Ajouter l'eau glacée petit à petit en

Orange Bread

Peel from 2 oranges, 1 cup sugar, 1 cup water, 3 cups flour, ½ tsp. salt, 3 tsp. baking powder, 1 egg, 1 cup milk, 1½ tbsp. melted butter.

Put the orange peel through the food chopper using the fine knife. Cover it with cold water and let it come to a boil. Drain. Add ½ cup sugar and the cup of water and cook them until thick, then cool. Sift the remaining dry ingredients. Add the beaten egg, milk, orange peel, and melted butter pan and bake in a moderate oven 1 hour.—B.C.

Today's Recipes

Bread Pudding—One cup bread crumbs, one cup sugar, three eggs, two and one-half cups milk. Beat the eggs, add two tablespoons butter, grated rind of one lemon, sugar and bread crumbs. Mix well and add milk. Pour into well buttered baking dish. Bake in moderate oven 350 degrees for 20 minutes.

Easter Glory Cake

Line bottoms of pans with paper; grease. Use two round 9-inch layer pans, 1½ inches deep. Start oven for moderate heat (375 degrees F.). Sift flour once before measuring. (All measurements are level).

Two and one quarter cups sifted cake flour, 3 tsp. double acting baking powder, 1 tsp. salt, 1½ cups sugar, ½ cup butter, ⅞ cup milk, 1 tsp. vanilla, 2 eggs, unbeaten.

Measure flour, baking powder, salt, and sugar into sifter. Stir shortening just to soften. Sift in dry ingredients. Add ¾ cup milk and the vanilla. Mix until flour is dampened. Then beat 300 strokes by hand, or 2 minutes in mixer (at a low speed). Add eggs and remaining milk. Beat 150 strokes by hand, or 1 minute in mixer (at a low speed). Count only actual beating strokes or time. (Scrape bowl and spoon or beater often). Turn batter into pans. Bake in moderate oven (375 degrees F.) about 25 minutes.

Gelatine Mix

Soak 1 tablespoon plain gelatine in ¼ cup cold water for 5 minutes. Scald 2 cups milk; dissolve the gelatine in it; cool to lukewarm. Cream 1 pound butter till it is the consistency of custard. Add the milk mixture. Mix slowly till the mixtures blend. If it separates keep on beating slowly and it will combine again. Pack in refrigerator butter dishes and keep chilled. This makes 2 pounds stretched butter.

Dumplings

Sift 1¼ cups of flour with ½ tsp. salt and 2 tsp. baking powder. Add 2/3 cup of milk, and 3 tbsp. of melted lard, to make a soft dough. Drop by spoonfuls into the stew.

INDEX

A

Acadian Pannacotta 182

Afishionado Fishmongers 179

Agnès's Doughnuts 210

apples
  Baked Apple Pudding 189
  Belliveau 185, 186, 212, 219
  Ben Davis 219, 221
  Cortland 223
  Cox Orange Pippin 219
  dehydrating 214
  Gravenstein 219, 223
  Honeycrisp 221
  MacIntosh 219
  Northern Spy 223
  Paula Red 219, 223
  Snow 219

Apples of Uncommon Character
    (Rowan Jacobsen) 221

A Taste of Acadie (Melvin Gallant and
    Marielle Cormier-Boudreau)
    12, 63, 146

B

Baie Sainte-Marie, La 3, 160, 185, 186,
    221

Baked Apple Pudding 189

Baking powder, tips on 22

beef 9, 128
  Aube Giroux's Classic French
      Canadian *Tourtière* 135
  Pâté à la viande 127

Marion Buoute's Meat Pie 130–131
  Tourtière 133

beets
  Chioggia 36, 38
  cider brine for 40
  pickled 37, 106
  preserving 40

Berenbaum, Rose Levy (*The Pie &
    Pastry Bible*) 215

Blancmange (Seaweed Pie) 178–79,
    181–82

blood, pig's. *See* pig, blood

boudin (blood sausage) 97, 109, 110,
    209

Boudreau, Chef Peter 146

Bran Bread 66

brawn. *See fromage à la tête de cochon*

bread
  Anadama 10, 68
  baking of 65
  Bran Bread 66
  challah 82
  cornbread. *See* Johnny Cakes
  Cornmeal and Molasses Sandwich
      Bread 68
  Cornmeal Sandwich Bread 72
  Good White Bread 82
  importance of 64–65
  Oat Bread 76
  Workhorse White Bread 79

Brown Sugar Sauce 190, 202

Buote, Melissa 131

butter, suggested use 22

Easy Caramel Sauce 177
Eaton, E. F. "Ted" (*Waste Not,
    Want Not*) 74
egg wash 136–37

F

fatback
    salted/curing of 87, 88, 90
flour
    Speerville 22
    suggested use of 22, 25
Folse, John 87
fricot xiv, 4, 15, 52, 121, 127, 139, 171
    Cajun *Fricot* 10, 121, 125
    Fricot aux poutines râpées 122
Fring Frangs 152, 154
fromage à la tête de cochon
        (headcheese) 97, 100, 106

G

Gallant, Melvin 12, 63, 146
Gâteau à la mélasse 173
Gillis, Goldie and Gilbert 179
Giroux, Aube 135
grand dérangement, le. See Deportation
Grand-Pré, NS 3, 199, 200
gratins (crackling) 91
Gravy (podcast) 125
guanciale 98

H

haddock 55, 149
    Seafood Chowder *à Mame* 160

Halifax Seaport Market 179
Hamilton, Gabrielle (*Prune*) 182
hare xvii, 89
    Fricot 121
    Pâté à la viande 127
headcheese. See *fromage à la tête de
        cochon*
Henderson, Fergus (*The Whole Beast*)
        101
hen, stewing 147
    Fricot aux poutines râpées 122
hops 63
Hutten, Anne (*Valley Gold*) 186
Hutten, Ted 212

I

Irish moss 178, 179, 180, 181, 182
    Blancmange 81

J

Johnny Cakes 74
Justinien's River. *See* Meteghan River

K

kids, baking with 176
Kitchen Vignettes 135

L

La Cuisine Acadienne d'Aujourd'hui
        (Les Dames Patronesses) 16, 76,
        111, 122, 146, 150–51, 163, 179,
        181, 206, 224

trotters 101
Pointe-de-l'Église, NS 56, 109, 118, 143
pollock 160
pork
    Aube Giroux's Classic French Canadian *Tourtière* 135
    confit 89
    fat xvii, xviii
    Marion Buote's Meat Pie 130–31
    sausage 125
    shoulder 134
Port Royal, NS 3, 221
potato
    Aube Giroux's Classic French Canadian *Tourtière* 135
    dumplings 122, 125
    in *fricot* 4, 121
    in yeast 63
    mashed 63, 110
    pancakes (*Fring Frangs*) 152, 154
    rappie pie 141, 143, 144, 146, 147, 148
    rasped 117, 118
    Seafood Chowder *à Mame* 160
    traditional use in Acadian food 139
poutines
    au lait vriou 186
    Québecois 139
    râpées 10–11, 121, 139, 140
preserving, tips on 34–35
Prince Edward Island 1, 2, 127, 146, 179, 209
    and meat pie 130
Pubnico, NS 56, 145

Q

quahog (*grosse coque*) 150
Québec xviii, 2, 4, 51, 127, 135, 163
Quinan, NS 144, 146

R

rabbit 128
rappie pie. *See* râpure
Rappie Pie Rules Facebook group 144
râpure (rappie pie) xiv, 7, 11, 52, 117, 127, 139, *142*, 143, 144
    German immigration and 140
    origins of 141, 143
rhubarb
    cooking with 44
    Rhubarb Chutney 44
    Rhubarb Conserves 6, 106, 182, 197
    Rhubarb Custard Pie 199–201
    pickled *32*, 43, 47
    Rhubarb Pudding 195
rillettes xviii, 89,163
Robichaud, Delbert (Robichaud's Meat Market) 109, 110

S

Saint Mary's Bay, NS. *See* Baie Sainte-Marie, La
salt fish 25, 87
salt pork 26
salt, use of 25
sauces
    cranberry 44, 117
    Brown Sugar Sauce 190, 202
    white sauce 4, 155, 157

OTHER COOKBOOKS
FROM NIMBUS

**OUT OF OLD NOVA
SCOTIA KITCHENS**
by Marie Nightingale
ISBN: 9781551099149

DUTCH OVEN (2ND EDITION)
by FMH Ladies Auxiliary
ISBN: 9781551099903

MARITIME FRESH
by Elisabeth Bailey
ISBN: 9781771080088

A REAL NEWFOUNDLAND SCOFF
by Liz Feltham
ISBN: 9781771082693